THEORY IN COST ACCOUNTING

THEORY IN COST ACCOUNTING

I. Narsis

ATLANTIC
PUBLISHERS & DISTRIBUTORS (P) LTD

Published by
ATLANTIC
PUBLISHERS & DISTRIBUTORS (P) LTD

Sales Office
7/22, Ansari Road, Darya Ganj,
New Delhi-110002
Phones : +91-11-23273880, 23275880, 23280451
Fax : +91-11-23285873
Web : www.atlanticbooks.com
E-mail : info@atlanticbooks.com

Branch Office
5, Nallathambi Street, Wallajah Road,
Chennai-600002
Phones : +91-44-64611085, 32413319
E-mail : chennai@atlanticbooks.com

Printed in India at Nice Printing Press, A-33/3A, Site-IV, Industrial Area, Sahibabad, Ghaziabad, U.P.

Preface

Cost Accounting can be described as the process of accumulating, measuring, analyzing, interpreting and reporting cost information that is both useful and relevant to the external stakeholders like banks, financial houses, investors, etc. and internal stakeholders such as company directors, managers, division heads, etc. In management accounting, cost accounting constitutes the part that establishes budget and actual cost operations, processes, analysis of variances, profitability or social use of funds.

The knowledge and understanding of cost accounting is an integral part of learning the overall nature of accounting and is one of the varied aspects of accounting available for careers in this field. Modernization of industry and its impact on globalization give much importance to cost accounting.

Cost accounting has long been used to help managers understand the costs of running a business. It originated during the industrial revolution when the complexities of running a large scale business led to the development of systems for recording and tracking costs to help business owners and managers make decisions. In the early industrial age, most of the costs incurred by a business were what modern accountants call 'variable costs' because they varied directly with the amount of production. Money was spent on labour, new materials and power to run a factory in direct proportion to the scale of production. Managers could simply add up the variable costs for a product and use this as a rough guide for decision-making processes. In modern cost accounting, the concept of recording history costs was taken further by allocating the company's fixed costs over a given period of time to the items produced during that period, and recording the result as the total cost of production.

Today, the managers use cost accounting to support decision making, reduce company's costs and improve its profitability. An important part of standard cost account is the variance analysis which breaks down the variation between actual cost and standard cost into different components so that managers can understand why costs were different from what was planned and take appropriate action to correct the situation. Cost accounting is being successfully implemented in service industries and non-profit organizations with encouraging results. This bears testimony to the fact that cost accounting is now vital to all 21st century businesses which face growing competition in the era of liberalization and globalization.

The book *Theory in Cost Accounting* concentrates on the theoretical aspect of concepts, methods and techniques of cost accounting, which are fundamental to the understanding of the discipline. It has been designed for B.Com., B.B.A., and M.Com. courses of various universities in India. It will be useful to the students, teachers, accountants, managers and businessmen.

I. Narsis

Contents

1

Cost Concept and Principles

1.1. EVOLUTION OF COST ACCOUNTING

Cost accounting is a recent development born in response to the needs of managers for detailed information about the cost of a product or service.

The characteristic features of modern industry, especially large-scale production, keen competition and complexity of the structure of production necessitated production of goods and services at the lowest possible cost. Production efficiency was considered to be the tool of profit maximisation. Losses and inefficiencies in the course of manufacture were sought to be eliminated or minimized by proper control measures at different points. Management became tremendously cost conscious.

Having become cost conscious, management was compelled to look for more and more detailed and day-to-day information, not only for ascertaining the actual cost of products, departments and processes, but also for control and reduction of cost. In spite of new accounting devices, improved techniques and procedures, financial information became inadequate for managerial ascertainment and control of costs. Cost accounting was evolved as a supplementary accounting method mainly for serving the needs of management. In the initial stages of its evolution, cost accounting was mainly concerned with product cost for cost ascertainment. Gradually there was a shift in emphasis to cost information for managerial control and foresight focusing on estimated and standard costing and is no longer confined to a postmortem examination of costs.

1.2. DEFINITION OF COST ACCOUNTING

"Costing is a study of the expenses incurred in manufacturing a product and conducting a business in such a manner that the expenses are analyzed and classified so as to enable the actual cost of any particular process or unit of production to be determined with a minimum of error."

The Institute of Costs and Management Accountants (ICMA) defines it as, "The application of the science, art and practice of cost control and the ascertainment of profitability. It includes the presentation of information derived therefrom for the purpose of managerial decision making."

1.3. OBJECT OF COSTING

Costing is a very useful to business management. It provides a technique for control of factoring and business operations. The following are the objects of costing:

1. To ascertain the actual cost of each article, process operation.
2. To locate profitable and unprofitable activities.
3. To serve as a guide in making estimates and preparing quotations for future.
4. To keep costs under control.
5. To find out the sources of waste and leakage.
6. To find out the efficiency and productive capacity of men and machines engaged in production.
7. To provide statistical data for formulation of business policies.
8. To provide sufficient information for budgetary control.
9. To find out the operative efficiency of each department and section.

1.4. COSTING PROCEDURE

Cost accounting is concerned with the transformation of financial accounting data. The activities that are included in the general term and their sequence are as below:

1. Classification: It is the grouping of costs according to their common characteristics. It is the process of analysis and identification of cost of comparable nature and/or arranging them into groups according to their patterns of behaviour, activities or processes.

2. Allocation: It is the charging of whole items of costs to suitable and identifiable cost centers or cost units. It is the transfer of the cost of a good or service, or the total of a group of such costs from primary account to one or more secondary accounts.

3. Apportionment: It is the distribution of a cost over several periods of time in proportion to anticipated benefits. It consists in dividing a joint or common cost or group of such costs between two or more cost objectives. This spread of overheads is an important but difficult operation and has generated a good deal of controversy in the cost accounting literature.

4. Absorption: It is the charging of items of cost to the ultimate cost units. It is the expensing of costs of job, product, process or unit, i.e. recovery by the product. The cost absorption process involves the recognition of expense under the conditions of: (a) physical movement, (b) benefit yielded, (c) period charge, etc.

1.5. CHARACTERISTICS OF A GOOD COSTING SYSTEM

An ideal system of costing should possess the following characteristics:

1. Accuracy: Cost accounts must be accurate and correct.

2. Equity: Allocation of overheads to a particular class of output, department or job should be fair and equitable.

3. Simplicity: The cost accounting system must be simple. It may be easy to understand. It must not involve heavy clerical labour. It must be such that even a new employee can easily understand it. In short it must be simple in record and simple to understand.

4. Elasticity: The costing system should be elastic and capable of being adjusted according to altered circumstances.

5. Economy: The cost of maintaining and running cost accounting system should be as low as possible. It must prove to be a profitable investment.

6. Comparability: The records must be maintained in such a manner that the results of one period can be compared with the results of any other period. The records of the past must act as a guide for the future.

7. Promptness: Prompt recording of the relevant figures in an analytical form is the sine quo non of costing.

8. Observance of instructions: The costing staff must carefully obey the instructions given to them. Even slight deviations from given instructions must not be permitted.

9. Periodical resulting: Costing results should be prepared periodically so that actual cost can be compared with estimated costs.

10. Reconciliation with financial accounts: The costing system should be so maintained as to make reconciliation with financial accounts easy and simple.

1.6. ADVANTAGES OF COST ACCOUNTING

1. Supplies detailed cost information: Cost accounting classifies cost and revenue by every possible division of the business and supplies management with detailed and regular cost information. Such information is of vital importance to management for ascertaining the cost of a product, process, department, division or unit of service.

2. Enables price fixation: Cost accounting helps asset management in fixation of selling price, not only during normal conditions of business, but also during a period of depression. On the basis of cost information supplied, it is possible to prepare estimates, tenders or quotations.

3. Discloses operating efficiency: Cost information reveals the relative profitability of various activities and enables management to put forth efforts to improve the operating efficiency of unprofitable lines, or consider the modification or elimination of such lines of activity.

4. Helps reveal idle capacity: Under-utilization of productive resources for reasons such as shortage of demand or bottlenecks in production, which result in idle plant and equipment is not only brought to light, but at the same time, enables management to ascertain the cost of idle capacity and modify its policy accordingly.

5. Facilitates planning: Besides analyzing and recording past costs and activities for product costing, cost accounting also enables management to know future costs so that appropriate plans and decisions can be made.

6. Guides decision-making: Decision-making is concerned with choosing between alternative courses of action. An important factor involved in the choice is the financial implication of the available alternatives. Cost accounting is a decision-making tool. It provides information to enable management to evaluate alternative courses of action.

7. Assists managerial control of costs: One of the functions of management is to ensure that operations, processes and costs are under control, and personnel in the organization are working efficiently towards achievement of organization goals. For this purpose, a concern will have a number of control systems, all depending upon detailed and timely cost information.

8. Helps financial accounting: The principle of matching costs and revenues under a modern cost accounting system is of great assistance to management in ascertaining the correct value of the closing inventory. Besides revealing the profit or loss of each line of activity, cost accounting also reveals the cause of any increase or decrease in the profit shown in the financial accounts. A good system of cost accounting provides a reliable check on the accuracy of financial accounting through reconciliation of profits.

9. Facilitates cost comparison: Cost accounting enables management to make cost comparison of jobs, products, departments, sales territories, etc. It renders possible not merely costs of different periods within the same concern but also inter-firm cost comparison.

10. Facilitates cost-plus contracting: While in the case of certain contracts, the contract price cannot be fixed, and the contractor is allowed a percentage of profit on actual cost, the information furnished by the cost accounting records is of immense use in fixation of the amount payable.

11. Assists adjustment of price: In the case of long-drawn contracts which provide for adjustment of agreed prices subject to escalation clause owing to change in cost consequent upon price fluctuations, cost information can conveniently be used for adjusting price and fixation of a new price.

12. Leads to new or improved methods: With a view to ensuring economical use of relatively scarce resources, management may, with the help of cost data, develop new or improved methods of production.

13. Preparation of income statement: Cost accounting enables management to prepare interim profit and loss account on a realistic basis, since cost records show the correct values of closing inventories.

14. Facilitates inter-firm comparison: Concerns in a particular industry, recording their costs uniformly, are enabled to submit the result to a trade association. Consequently, information of the utmost value to the members can be exchanged without prejudice to the interest of individual members.

1.7. LIMITATIONS OF COST ACCOUNTING

Cost accounting suffers from certain inherent limitations. These limitations are as follows:

1. Absence of readymade system: There is no stereotyped system of cost accounting applicable to all industries and even firms in the same industry. A suitable system, which is workable, should be designed taking into consideration all the relevant factors in its installation. The flexibility in introduction involves the human element, and is equally so in its working. Consequently, the system may prove a failure if the techniques of cost accounting are not properly handled.

2. Cost differences: While the principles of cost accounting are the same regardless of the nature of business, the principles themselves keep on changing. Further, there is bound to be divergence in cost accounting procedures. For instance, though the distinction between direct and indirect materials is one of principle, what is considered to be direct material in one concern may be indirect in the case of another because of different management policies. The same is true of fixed and variable overheads and controllable and uncontrollable overheads.

3. Varied cost concepts: There are, in practice, widely recognized cost concepts but understood and applied differently by different concerns. Since different costs are used for different purposes, no one cost is suitable for all purposes. For instance, actual costs are different from standard costs and both are different from estimated costs and decision-making costs. Similarly, factory expenses, a term used for factory overhead, is considered to be a misnomer, since the same is a part of product cost and becomes an expense only when the goods are sold. Such terminological differences are bound to introduce confusion. Although confusion may be avoided by making certain assumptions, the results arrived at by two cost accountants are bound to be different.

4. Empirical science: It has already been pointed out that cost accounting is an empirical science, distilled from experience. Further, the introduction and success of any system of cost accounting depends upon the human factors. As such, if the system introduced proves a failure, the system itself cannot be blamed. This is obvious from the fact that this discipline is not an exact science and its postulates cannot be verified by controlled experiment, but only by application in actual practice.

1.8. COSTING TECHNIQUES

There are different techniques of costing to be used in any method of costing. The following are the important techniques of costing:

1. Uniform costing: It is the use of the same costing principles by several concerns for common control or comparison of costs.

2. Marginal costing: It is the ascertainment of marginal cost. It is used to ascertain effects of changes in volume or type of output on profit.

3. Budgetary control: It involves the fixation of budgets or estimated cost and comparison of actual cost with the budgets fixed.

4. Standard costing: A comparison is made of the actual cost with a pre-arranged standard and the cost of any deviations is analysed by causes. This enables the management to investigate the reasons for these deviations and to take suitable corrective action.

1.9. INSTALLING COSTING SYSTEM

A good system of costing serves as a means of control over expenditure and helps to secure economy in manufacture. It is an integral part of a good management. While introducing a costing system for the following general or preliminary steps should be taken:

1. The technical details of the business should be carefully studied. The technical staff should be consulted.
2. A suitable costing system should be adopted to suit the general organization of the particular business.
3. The details in which records are to be kept should be arranged.
4. Standard printed forms should be provide wherever possible and they should be numbered for control purposes.
5. Arrangements should be made for the prompt availability of cost information.
6. An efficient system of material control should be introduced in order to impose a rigid check on the purchasing, storage and issue of materials and stores.
7. A well defined system of wage procedure should be introduced to control the cost of labour.
8. A sound plan should be devised for the collection, allocation, appointment and absorption of overheads.

9. The degree of accuracy desired should be determined.
10. The technique of budgetary control should be introduced for comparing the actual performance with budgeted performance.
11. The system of financial accounting should be carefully examined. It should be enquired if it is possible to incorporate cost accounts in financial accounts. If this is not possible, the costing system should be so devised that its results are capable of easy reconciliation with those of financial accounts.

1.10. DIFFICULTIES IN INSTALLATION

Following are the difficulties in installing costing system:

1. Lack of co-operation from other executives.
2. Suspicion of workers and their resistance to the installation of the system.
3. Lack of cost consciousness and absence of interest reducing the cost.
4. The forms and other records may not be properly maintained and submitted to cost office. In order to overcome these practical difficulties, the following steps should be taken:
   (i) Workers confidence in the system should be gained before its introduction.
   (ii) Regular meetings should be organized to clear their doubts its introduction.
   (iii) The executives should be explained the benefits which they will derive from the system in the discharge of their duties.
   (iv) After installation also, continuous check over the progress of the system should be kept. It is only through the continuous efforts of a cost accountant that the system will turn out successful and the objects may be achieved.

1.11. NATURE OF COST ACCOUNTING

Cost accounting is an organized body of knowledge. It consists of certain principles and rules to which the technique of costing should be applied. These principles and rules have been developed over a period of time by experience. That is why, according to Bigg, "Costing is an empirical science, that is to say, the rules which govern it are largely conditioned by the operations, personnel, and policy of the undertaking with respect to which its techniques are to be applied."

Besides being a science, cost accounting is also an art. The priciples, rules and techniques governing cost accounting are not static but dynamic. They change with the passage of time: old principles and techniques, which become outmoded, are replaced by new ones. Besides laying down rules for cost accumulation and presentation, it also shows the way of achieving the purposes for which it is installed. Again, the introduction of sophisticated techniques in the field of cost accounting renders the discipline to be called an art also.

1.12. SCOPE OF COST ACCOUNTING

Cost accounting is concerned with the ascertainment and control of costs. It provides management with information relating to the financial aspects of performance of an enterprise. The information thus provided enables management to perform functions such as planning, control and decision-making efficiently.

In the initial stages of its evolution, cost accounting confined itself to accumulation of historical costs and presentation of the same for the sole purpose of cost finding or product costing. With the passage of time, however, its scope was broadened and provision became more important than product costing.

Besides the enlargement of its scope, the extent of its application has also become wider. Confined only to manufacturing organizations application in a number of diverse organizations such as transport undertakings, printing industry, hospitals, educational institutions, governmental agencies, local authorities, farms, extractive industries, banks and insurance companies.

1.13. FINANCIAL ACCOUNTING AND COST ACCOUNTING

Similarity

1. Recording is accomplished in both with the same basic documents.
2. Information is recorded in both in terms of money.
3. The principles of debit and credit are common to both.
4. Both show cost and profit.

Distinction

Financial Accounting	Cost Accounting
1. Financial accounts are the accounts of the whole business.	1. Cost accounts are only a part of the financial accounts.
2. The costs are reported in total in this account.	2. The costs are broken down on a unit basis in these accounts.
3. These relate to all commercial transactions of the business.	3. They relate to transactions connected with the manufacture of goods and services.
4. They deal with actual facts and figures.	4. They deal with estimates and standards.
5. They are concerned with external transactions.	5. They are concerned with internal transactions.
6. Financial accounts disclose the net profit or loss of the business.	6. They disclose profit or loss of each product unit, etc.
7. They include all expenses, viz. manufacturing, office, selling and non-cost items.	7. They include only those expenses when enter into production.

Financial Accounting	Cost Accounting
8. Stock is valued at cost or market price whichever is less.	8. Stock in valued at cost.
9. It does not reveal material wastage and idle time.	9. It reveals wastages and idle time.
10. Preparation of interim Profit & Loss Account and Balance Sheet is not possible.	10. Preparation of interim Profit & Loss Account and Balance Sheet is possible.
11. Inter-period and Inter-firm comparison is not possible.	11. Comparison is possible.
12. For important managerial decisions data is insufficient.	12. For important managerial decisions data is sufficient.
13. It is a postmortem analysis.	13. It is not a postmortem analysis.
14. Financial accounts necessarily form part of the double entry process.	14. Cost accounts do not form part of the ordinary process of double entry.
15. Financial accounting lays emphasis on the double entry process.	15. Cost accounting provides for a detailed system of control with the help to standard costing and budgetary control.
16. Financial accounts have to be prepared according to the requirements of Companies Act and Income-tax Act.	16. Maintenance of cost accounts is not compulsory. It is purely voluntary.

1.14. MANAGEMENT ACCOUNTING AND COST ACCOUNTING

Distinction

1. Cost accounting provides just cost information for managerial purposes, while management accounting provides all accounting information, i.e. not merely cost information but financial information as well.
2. The scope of management accounting is much wider than that of cost accounting. Relatively, therefore, management accounting uses more advanced techniques of management reporting.
3. In providing cost information, cost accounting uses financial information provided by financial accounting by classifying the expenses under heads of performance, after minutely dissecting every item of expenditure. Management accounting uses both cost and financial information.
4. Cost accounting evolved out of financial accounting, while management accounting evolved out of cost accounting.
5. The main purpose of cost accounting is that reporting of current and prospective costs of product, service, department, job, process and operations. It is oriented towards managerial control of current and future operations of an enterprise. Management accounting, on the other hand, is concerned with the provision of accounting information to management at all levels for the purpose of formulation of policies, planning, execution of plans, and thereby ensure maximization of profit.
6. The cost accountant is interested in preparing budgets, setting standards, measuring actual performance with the set standards and reporting significant deviations for necessary action, besides cost ascertainment. However, the management accountant will go a step further in making variance analysis and suggesting ways and

means of improving the efficiency of operations. He concentrates his attention on matters relating to finance, profitability and productivity.

7. While stewardship accounting led to the evolution of cost accounting, a sound system of cost accounting led to the evolution of management accounting.
8. While cost accounting may also be called 'control accounting', management accounting may be called 'decision-making accounting'.

1.15. COST SHEET

The analysis for the different elements of cost of the product is shown in the form of a statement called "Cost Sheet". Cost sheet is a schedule or document which provides for the presentation of the estimated detailed cost in respect of a cost centre or a cost unit. It is only a memorandum statement and is not a part of the double entry cost accounts. The statement summaries the cost of manufacturing a particular list of product and discloses:

1. the prime cost,
2. the works cost,
3. the cost of production, and
4. the total cost.

When the department cost is divided by the number of units produced, the quotient is the average cost per unit of the work performed. Separate columns could be provided for the total and the unit cost of each element of cost. Columns could also be drawn for the current and the past periods. Cost sheet is prepared at weekly, monthly, or other intervals.

Performa of Cost Sheet

Specimen of Cost Sheet

COST SHEET FOR THE PERIOD________________

Production________________Units

	Total Cost	*Cost per unit*
Direct Materials:		
Opening stock...	xx	
Purchases...	xx	
Carriage inwards...	xx	
Less: Closing stock...	xx	
Direct materials consumed	xx	
Direct wages	xx	
Direct expenses	xx	
Prime Cost:		xxx
Add: **Works or factory Overheads:**		
Indirect materials	xx	
Indirect wages	xx	
Rent and rates (factory)	xx	
Lighting and heating	xx	
Power and fuel	xx	
Repairs and maintenance	xx	
Cleaning	xx	
Drawing office expenses	xx	
Cost of Research and experiments	xx	
Depreciation of factory plant	xx	
Works stationery	xx	
State insurance	xx	
Welfare service expenses	xx	
Insurance-Fixed assets etc.		
Works manager's salaries etc.	xx	
Works or Factory Cost:		xxx

Add: Office and Administrative Overheads:		
Rent and rates	xx	
Salaries	xx	
Lighting and heating	xx	
Insurance	xx	
Cleaning	xx	
Telephone and postages	xx	
Printing and Stationery	xx	
Depreciation of furniture and office equipments and buildings	xx	
Legal expenses	xx	
Audit fees	xx	
Bank charges	xx	
Cost of Production:		
Add: Selling and Distribution Overheads:		
Showroom rent and rates	xx	
Lighting and heating	xx	
Salesmen's salaries	xx	
Commission	xx	
Traveling expenses of salesman	xx	
Sales printing and stationary	xx	
Advertising	xx	
Bad debts	xx	
Director in charge (sales)	xx	
Postage	xx	
Depreciation and expenses of delivery van		
Carriage freight outwards	xx	
Samples and other free gifts	xx	
Cost of Sales:		xx
Add (or deduct) Net Profit (or loss)		xx
Sales		xx

Note: Items of expenses which are an appropriation of profit should not form a part of the costs. Examples of such expenses are:

(i) Income Tax; (ii) Dividends to shareholders; (iii) Commission to Managing Directors or Partners; (iv) Capital loss, i.e. loss arising out of sale of assets; (v) Interest on loan, (vi) Donations; (vii) Capital expenditure; (viii) Discount on shares and Debentures; (ix) Underwriting commission; (x) Writing off goodwill.

1.16. COST ACCOUNTING CONCEPTS

1. Cost: Cost is the amount of expenditure incurred on a given thing. Cost represents the resources that have been or must be sacrificed to attain a particular objective. For instance, cost of making a table comprises sums spent on materials like wood, nails, polish, wages paid to carpenter and other expenses.

2. Costing: Costing has been defined as the technique and process of ascertaining costs. (I.C.M.A. London, *Terminology of Cost Accountancy*). It involves systems, methods and techniques of accumulation, classification, analysis and appropriate allocation of expenditure incurred in respect of a product or service.

3. Cost accounting/Cost accountancy: The Institute of Costs and Management Accounts (ICMA) defines it as, "The application of costing and cost accounting principles, methods and techniques to the science, art and practice of cost control and the ascertainment of profitability. It includes the presentation of information derived therefrom for the purpose of managerial decision making."

4. Cost unit: Since cost ascertainment is the central activity in cost accounting, the ascertainment of cost necessitates the determination of unit in terms of which costs can be ascertained and expressed. The unit of product or service chosen as the unit for costing purposes is known as a cost unit.

5. Cost centre: For administrative convenience, every large-scale business is usually divided into a number of departments such as production, marketing and finance. These departments represent the basic functions of any business and each of these functions consists of distinct activities.

Examples of Cost Units

Product or Industry	Cost unit
Confectionery	One kg. or one batch
Engineering	One job or one batch
Jobbing industry	One job
Bakery	One kg. or one pound
Typewriter	One Typewriter
Radio	One Radio or one batch
Television	One Television or one batch
Medicine	One batch
Refrigerator	One Refrigerator
Automobile	One Car or one batch
Cement	One bag or tonne
Coal	One tonne
Printing	One job
Pencil	One gross
Bricks	One thousand
Slates	One gross or thousand
Steel	One tonne
Gas	One cubic metre
Chemicals	One litre kg. or tonne
Brewery	A bottle or a crate
Canteen	One meal
Hospital	Patient-bed or patient-night
Electricity	Kilowatt-hours
Transport	Tonne-km or passenger-km
Nuts and Bolts	kg. or gross
Buildings	One contract
Ships	One ship

For the purpose of accumulating costs and charging the same to cost units, these departments are further divided into smaller sections, each of which is known as a cost center.

The production activities of an oil milling industry may also be divided into distinct parts such as crushing, refining and finishing. Each of these production lines or processes forms one cost center.

6. Service cost centers: With a view to serving the needs of those who are engaged in the main activities of production, selling and distribution, and thereby ensure smooth and efficient running of the business, management creates service departments. Departments such as payroll, purchase, personnel, power house, maintenance, etc. are as important and necessary as production and marketing departments. Besides their practical importance, service departments also involve heavy costs. It is, therefore, necessary to ascertain the cost of service and control the same efficiently. For this purpose, service cost the cost, of a service cost center is charged to production cost centers on an equitable basis.

2

Elements of Cost

2.1. VARIOUS ELEMENTS OF COST

The cost of manufacturing a product is sub-divided into what are known as elements of cost. Thus, elements of cost are the primary classification of costs according to the factors upon which expenditure is incurred. The elements of cost consist of material, labour and expenses. Each element can again be divided into direct and indirect items or costs.

1. Materials: The substances from which the products are made are known as materials. They may be in a raw or manufactured state. They can be direct as well as indirect.

Direct materials: Direct materials are those materials which can be identified in the product and can be conveniently measured and directly charged to the product. Thus, these materials directly enter the product and form a part of the finished product. The examples are timber in furniture making, cloth in dress making, bricks in building a house.

Indirect materials: Indirect materials are those materials which do not normally form a part of the finished product. They are defined as "materials which cannot be allocated but which can be apportioned to or absorbed by cost centers or cost units". The examples are lubricants, cotton waste, grease, oils, small tools, etc.

2. Labour: For conversion of materials into finished goods, human effort is needed. Such human effort is called labour. Labour can be direct as well as indirect.

Direct labour: Labour which takes an active and direct part in the production of a particular commodity is called direct labour. Wages of such labour are known as direct wages.

Indirect labour: Labour employed for the purpose of carrying out work incidental to goods or services provided is indirect labour. Such labour do not alter the construction, composition or condition of the product. Wages of foremen, store-keepers, time-keepers, salaries to salesmen, director's fees, etc. are all examples of indirect labour costs.

3. **Expenses:** Expenses may be direct or indirect.

Direct expenses: These are expenses which can be directly, conveniently and wholly allocated to cost centers or cost units. Examples of direct expenses are: cost of special drawings, tools made for a specific product, the hire of special tools required by a particular job.

Indirect expenses: These are expenses which cannot be directly, conveniently and wholly allocated to cost centers or cost units. Indirect expenses can be classified into three categories:

(a) Manufacturing expenses: These are also called works or factory or production expenses. Such expenses which are incurred in the factory and are concerned with the running of the factory are known as manufacturing expenses. Examples are: rent, rates and insurance of factory premises; power used in factory, depreciation of factory building, plant and machinery, etc.

(b) Office expenses: These are also called administrative expenses or office overheads. Such expenses which are incurred known as office expenses. Examples are office rent, light and heat, postage and telegrams, bank charges, legal charges, audit-fee, depreciation of office building, furniture, etc.

(c) Selling and distribution expenses: Expenses incurred for marketing of a commodity, for securing orders for the goods, and for making efforts to find and retain customers are called selling and distribution expenses. Examples are: advertisement expenses, traveling expenses, bad debts, collection charges, etc.

2.2. CHART SHOWING THE CLASSIFICATION OF EXPENSES

Direct Materials :
Direct Labour : = Prime Cost
Direct Expanses :
Prime Cost Plus Factory Expenses:
Indirect Materials :
Indirect Labour : = Factory Cost
Indirect Expenses :
Factory Cost plus
Administrative Expenses : = Total Cost
Selling Expenses : or
Distribution : Cost of Sales
Expenses :
Total Cost:
Plus Profit :
or : = Selling Price
Minus Loss :

2.3. INTERCHANGEABLE WORDS

General Terms	Interchangeable with
Prime Cost	Flat cost; first cost; direct cost.
Factory Cost	Works cost; production cost; manufacturing cost.
Cost of Production	Office cost; gross cost.
Cost of Sales	Selling cost; total cost; distribution cost.
Factory Oncost	A charge to be made against each job to cover miscellaneous expenses, e.g. cleaning; experiments.
Office Oncost	Administration expenses such as rent; salaries; management costs.
Overhead Charges	A term applied to any item comprising oncost.

2.4. COMPONENTS OF TOTAL COST

Functionally, the main divisions or components of the total cost of a product are: prime cost, works cost, works cost, cost of production, cost of sales, and selling price. These, in fact, symbolize the successive stages through which costs flow.

(a) **Prime cost:** Prime cost is the aggregate of direct materials cost, direct wages and variable direct expenses. It is also known as flat cost or direct cost or basic cost or first cost.

(b) **Works cost:** Works cost represents prime cost plus a proportion of works or factory expenses properly chargeable against its production. It is also known as factory cost or manufacturing cost or mill cost or production cost or foundry cost or cost of manufacture.

(c) **Office cost:** Office cost represents works cost plus a proportion of office and administrative expenses. It is also known as gross cost or cost production or value of output or cost of output.

(d) **Total cost:** Total cost is the sum of all the items of expenditure incurred in producing and distributing any product. It comprises works cost plus proportion of office and administration cost, and proportion of selling and distribution expenses properly chargeable to that product. It is also known as final cost or selling cost or cost of turnover.

2.5. COST CLASSIFICATION

In simple language, classification may be defined as the process of arranging items into groups according to their common characteristics or degree of similarity. The Terminology defines classification as: "The arrangement of items in logical groups having regard to their nature (subjective classification) or the purpose to be fulfilled (objective classification)."

The following are the different methods of cost classification:

1. Elements: The cost elements of a product or its components are materials, labour and expenses. This classification provides management with information necessary for product pricing and income measurement.

Materials. According to the Terminology, Material cost is the cost of commodities, other than fixed assets, introduced into products or consumed in the operation of an organisation. Materials are the principal substances used in production, and these are transformed into finished goods. They are distinguished as direct and indirect materials.

Direct materials. The Terminology defines direct material cost as elements of a product or saleable service. Thus, materials which can be identified with the production of a product or which can be traced to the finished product are known as direct materials.

Cotton in the production of cloth, leather in the production of leather goods, oilseeds in the production of oil, wood in the production of paper and matches, lime in the production of chalk, etc. are some examples of direct materials.

Indirect materials. According to the Terminology, Material cost, other than direct material cost, is known as indirect material cost. Accordingly, materials used in the production of a product that are not direct materials, are known as indirect materials. In other words, material cost which cannot be identified with a product, job or process, or traceable to the same, is known as indirect material cost.

Materials required for operating and maintaining plant and equipment, small tools, works stationery, etc. are some examples of indirect materials.

Labour. Labour is the physical or mental effort expended in production. The remuneration for such efforts is known as wages. Labour cost or wages is defined by the Terminology as "the cost of employees remuneration". Labour is also distinguished as direct and indirect.

Direct wages. According to Wheldon, "Direct wages are incurred in altering the construction, composition, conformation or condition of the product." This definition implies that all labour, whether skilled or unskilled, engaged on a job or process is direct provided the labour time spent on the same can be ascertained and the money value of such time can be charged to the job concerned.

Indirect wages. Indirect wages cost is the remuneration paid to workers who do not work directly on a product or saleable service. While the wages paid to workers to transform raw materials and components into finished product are direct salaries of foremen, inspector, store-keeper, production control staff, maintenance wages, idle time, etc. are treated as indirect wages.

Expenses. As one of the elements of cost, the term 'expenses' denotes the cost of services provided to an undertaking. Pointing out that this is a specialized term used in costing, some authors prefer the usage of singular number, distinguishing it from its plural number 'expenses' which, according to them, denotes payment for wages and outlay upon the purchase of goods and services of all kinds.

Direct expenses. Expenses may also be classified as direct and indirect. According to the Terminology, "Direct expenses are all costs other than materials nor of direct labour but are specifically incurred for a particular job or process and, as such chargeable to it".

Hire charges of special plant or tool, cost of special patterns or designs royalty paid per unit of a copyright design, hire of a crane for a specific contract, etc. are the examples of direct expenses.

Indirect expenses. According to the Terminology, indirect expenses are "expenses, other than direct expenses". Factory rent and rates, insurance of plant and machinery, power, light, heating, repairs, telephone, etc. are some examples of indirect expenses.

2. Identifiably: Costs may also be classified as direct and indirect on the basis of the relationship with the cost center or cost unit. Direct costs are those that can be identified with and allocated to cost centers or cost units. Indirect costs are those that cannot be identified with and allocated, but which can be apportioned to cost centers or cost units.

Direct costs may be sub-divided into direct material cost, direct labour cost and direct expenses. Similarly, indirect costs may be sub-divided into indirect materials cost, indirect labour cost and indirect expenses.

3. Relationship to production: Costs may also be classified according to their relationship to production. On this basis, we may distinguish between prime cost and conversion cost. Prime cost is the sum of direct material cost, direct expenses. Conversion cost is the cost of processing materials into finished products. These costs include direct wages and factory overhead.

4. Functions: Costs may also be classified on the basis of business functions, viz. according to the purpose for which they are incurred. When costs are grouped according to broad divisions of business activity, costs are accumulated on the basis of activity performed.

On this basis, we may distinguish production or manufacturing cost, administration cost, selling cost, distribution cost and research addition to manufacturing activities, costs may also arise in relation to them.

5. Relationship to volume: The relationship between cost and output, known as the 'cost function', is also one of the methods of classifying costs. A change in the level of activity or volume, other things being equal, brings about a change in costs. Thus, on the basis of behavior of costs, we may distinguish fixed, variable and semi-variable costs.

Fixed costs are those that remain constant over a certain output limit, and vary beyond that limit. Even within the output limit, fixed costs remain constant in total, while the cost per unit varies with the output. These costs are also known as period costs or committed costs since they will be incurred in advance of production, and will not be affected by the volume of activity. In the long run, if the output limit is exceeded, they change in total and cease to be fixed.

Variable costs, on the other hand, tend to change in total indirect proportion to changes in volume or output, while the cost per unit remains constant. The Terminology defines variable cost as: "A cost which, in the aggregate, tends to vary in direct proportion to changes in the volume of output or turnover."

Semi-variable costs contain both fixed and variable elements. They are neither wholly fixed nor wholly variable. As such, they are known as mixed costs. Telephone service charges, for instance, comprise a fixed rental charge regardless of the number of calls, and the variable element of charge per call. Similarly, fixed supervision charges for a given number of operatives to be supervised, and increase in the supervision charge when the number of operatives to be supervised, and increase in the supervision charge when the number of operatives is increased. In the latter case, the term 'stepped cost' is also used.

6. Departments: A major functional division of a business is known as a department. Costing by departments helps management to control overhead cost and measure income. When classified on the basis of departments, we distinguish between production department costs and service department costs.

Production departments contribute directly to the production of goods.

Manual and machine operation performed on the product take place in the production departments, and inputs are transformed into output. The function of service departments is to provide services to the production departments. Accordingly, they are not directly related to the production of an item. The costs of these departments are apportioned to the production department, since the latter benefit from the services of the former.

7. Controllability: Costs may be classified according to whether their amount can be influenced by management, or whether the level of costs is determined by external factors. If it is possible to hold a manager responsible for the increase in costs, they may be classified on the basis of the area of responsibility.

Thus, costs incurred in a particular responsibility center, and amenable to control by the managerial personnel of that center are known as controllable costs. Uncontrollable costs, on the other hand, are those that cannot be influenced by management, although incurred in a responsibility center.

8. Time of computation: On the basis of the time of computing costs, costs are classified as historical costs and pre-determined costs. Historical costs are those that are computed following the incurring of advance of production. A predetermined cost may either be an estimated cost or standard cost. Estimated costs, which are less scientific than standard costs, are used to evaluate performance by a comparison with the actuals.

9. Period charged to income: Costs may also be classified on the basis of when they are to be charged against revenues. Some costs are first recorded as assets and later charged to revenue, while others are straightaway recorded as expenses. Accordingly, distinction is drawn between product costs and period costs. This distinction is of considerable importance to management for income measurement and matching expenses to revenues in the proper period.

10. Normality: From the point of view of cost control, it is also possible to distinguish between normal costs and abnormal costs. If costs are well within the target fixed in the budget or plan, they are considered to be normal, and if they exceed the budgeted level, they are analysed as abnormal. Abnormal costs can be controlled if identified at an early stage.

11. Decision-making costs: Managerial decisions, involving choosing the most economically desirable course of action from amongst alternative courses of action, are facilitated by distinguishing decision-marking costs. The types of cost used in this context are: marginal costs, differential costs, opportunity costs, replacement costs, out-of-pocket costs, sunk costs, imputed costs, shutdown costs, etc.

2.6. METHOD OF COSTING

Basically there are two methods of costing, namely, (a) job costing and (b) process costing. Job costing is suitable for industries manufacturing different products or executing different jobs for different customers according to different specifications. Process costing is suitable for industries where production is continuous and units are identical.

All other methods of costing are improvements, extensions or combinations of job costing and process costing. The following are the important methods of costing:

1. Job costing: This method is also called job-order costing. This refers to a system of costing in which costs are ascertained in terms of specific jobs or orders. The unit of cost is individual order from a customer or it may consist of products manufactured for keeping them in stock for eventual sale. This method is suitable for printers, construction engineers, motor repair workshops, etc.

2. Contract costing: This method is also called terminal costing. This method of costing is suitable to contractors who receive definite orders for execution. Contract costing discloses the accurate cost of each contract, from time to time, during the course of its completion. This method can be applied to contract business, engineering works, ship building, etc.

3. Batch costing: This is a form of job costing. Certain factories may have to produce a number of parts to make a product. Such factories undertake production of each part in batches. The cost of each batch can be ascertained by applying the batch costing. This method is mainly applied in biscuit manufacture. Garments manufacture spare parts and components manufacture.

4. Unit costing: This method is also called output or single costing. This method is suitable for industries where method manufacture is continuous and units are identical. It is a simple method of costing in which the total cost is divided by the number of units produced to determine the cost per unit. The method is applied to industries like mines, quarries, oil drilling, breweries cement works, brick works, etc.

5. Process costing: In the manufacture of some commodities the raw material passes through different stages or process before it takes the shape of final product. Each process is distinct and expenses can be conveniently allocated to each process. The product of the first process or stage becomes the raw material of the second stage, and the product of the second stage becomes the raw material of the third stage. In such industries, process costing is employed. The manufacturer can find out the cost of each process. The process costing is a method of costing which is employed where production involves several process which are distinct and independent of each other. Process costing is generally followed in textile industries, chemical industries, tanneries paper manufacture, etc.

6. Departmental costing: When a factory is divided into a number of departments. It is desirable to ascertain the cost of operating each department. For this purpose, departmental costing is introduced. Departmental costing is usually associated with output costing.

7. Operating cost: This is a method of costing used to find out the cost of performing a service. This system, therefore, is applied to those undertakings which perform some service rather than producing a commodity. This system is suitable for rail and road transport services, electricity supplying companies, hospitals, water works, gas companies canteens, etc.

8. Multiple costing: This is also known as composite costing. This involves the application of more than one method of costing in respect of the same product. For example, process costing may be applied up to a certain stage and then job costing may be used. Thus, multiple costing is a combination of two or more methods. Examples of industries in which this method is used are cycle manufacture, motor car manufacture, aeroplanes, machine tools, radios, typewriters, etc.

Besides the above methods, there are three special methods of costing which are used by management only for controlling costs and making some important managerial decisions. They are: (a) uniform costing; (b) marginal costing; and (c) standard costing.

3

Material

3.1. DIRECT MATERIAL

All those basic raw materials which are used in the manufacture of a particular article are direct materials. Direct materials physically enter into the production process and become a part of the finished product. For example, cotton used in textile mills, timber used in furniture, steel used in manufacturing machines, etc.

3.2. INDIRECT MATERIAL

Indirect materials are those materials which do not normally form a part of the finished product. It simply helps the production process. For example, nails used in furniture, fuel oil and waste, polish, etc.

3.3. DEFINITION OF MATERIAL CONTROL

The regulation of the functions of an organization relating to the procurement, storage, and usage of materials in such a way as to maintain an even flow of production without excessive investment in material stock.

3.4. OBJECTIVES OF MATERIAL CONTROL

The twin objectives of material control are: (a) maintenance of even flow of production, and (b) prevention of excessive investment in material stock, the objectives, confliction as they can be reconciled by outlining the following objectives:

1. To effect purchases of materials of the right quality consistent with the standards prescribed in respect of the finished product.
2. To procure materials on the most favorable terms with a view to effecting maximum economy in the cost of buying.
3. To make available an assured supply of materials so as to keep the cycle of production going without any interruption.
4. To ensure effective utilization of materials.
5. To prevent over-stocking of materials and the consequent locking-up of working capital.
6. To prevent losses during storage of materials.
7. To provide management with information regarding the cost of materials, and the availability of stock.

3.5. NEED FOR MATERIAL CONTROL

Material control aims at achieving saving in material cost improvement in material handling, increased production and larger profits. It ensures:

1. Timely availability of right type of material resulting in smooth and continuous flow of production.
2. Purchase of stores of appropriate quality at reasonable price.
3. Minimum capital investment in the inventory by fixing stock levels and avoiding over stocking.
4. Economy in buying and holding expenses by evolving an ideal order quantity for each item.
5. Prevention of lockage, deterioration, wastage of material by arranging suitable storage facilities and by fixing allowable limits of such losses in storing as well as manufacturing.
6. Minimization of risk due to spoilage, obsolescence, theft, pilferage by enforcing stock control measures and physical verification of stock.

7. Saving to material consumption by reviewing and revising product design.
8. Correct measurement of deficiency in material consumption by calculating material turnover, input output ratio, etc.
9. Maintenance of appropriate stock records which furnish the date relating to stores quickly and accurately.

3.6. ESSENTIALS OF MATERIAL CONTROL

The following are the essentials of a good system of material control:

1. There should be proper co-operation between various departments which are involved in purchasing, receiving, inspecting, storing and accounting materials.
2. There should be centralized purchasing under the control of a trained purchasing agent.
3. There should be proper planning of material requirements.
4. There should be proper classification of materials with codes, materials with codes, material standardization and simplification.
5. There should be planned physical as well as efficient book control through satisfactory storage control procedures.
6. There should be proper storage of materials and properly safeguard under supervision.
7. Appropriate records should be maintained to control issue and utilization of stores in production.
8. There should be a system of perpetual inventory so that it is possible at any moment to find out the quantity and value of materials in stock.
9. There should be an efficient system of internal audit and internal check.
10. Maximum, minimum and recording level of stocks should be fixed.

11. There should be a system of regular reporting to management regarding materials purchased storage and utilization.

3.7. ADVANTAGES OF MATERIAL CONTROL

The following are the advantages of material control:

1. It eliminates waste in the use of materials.
2. It reduces the risk of loss from fraud and theft.
3. It helps in keeping perpetual inventory and other records to facilitate the preparation of accurate material reports to the management.
4. It reduces the cost of storage.
5. It reduces the capital tied up in materials.
6. It provides accurate information about the value of materials used in various departments.
7. It prevents production delays due to lack of materials by supplying required quantities at the right time.

3.8. STEPS IN PURCHASING PROCEDURE

Purchasing is a specialist activity and it is carried on by a separate department under the control of a purchasing officer purchasing is of extreme importance to manufacturing concerns. Therefore, purchasing officer in a manufacturing concern has considerable responsibility. It is by his department that much money can be saved or lost. The purchasing officer requires good technical knowledge of the industry. He must have constant touch with market prices, reports and market trends. He should have a working knowledge of contract law and procedure. He should have up-to-date knowledge of government policies regarding export and import restrictions and various duties and taxes.

3.9. FUNCTIONS OF THE PURCHASING DEPARTMENT

The following are the functions of the purchasing department:

1. Receiving purchase requisitions: The first function of the purchasing officer is to receive duly authorized purchase requisitions from various departments. Purchases should not be permitted unless duly authorized purchase requisitions are received. Purchase requisition is a document which authorizes the purchasing department to purchase materials. The purchasing officer places orders for goods in accordance with the requisitions received from (i) the storekeeper, (ii) the production control department, (iii) the plant and maintenance engineer, and (iv) the head of the department.

2. Studying the market and sources of supply: Having decided to purchase materials, the purchasing officer should know where and when prices are favorable. He must have the full information about the sources of supply of materials and details of the manufacturers. The purchasing officer obtains the necessary information from past records, catalogues, price list, etc. For big requirements he should invite tenders, and for regular requirement he can negotiate a rate.

3. Issuing purchase orders: After deciding about the source of supply, the next function of the purchasing officer is to prepare purchase order. It is a request made by the purchaser to supplier to deliver certain goods of requisite quality and quantity at the terms and conditions agreed upon. Once the purchase order is sent to the supplier, it is a commitment on the part of the purchaser to accept delivery and make payment. This purchase order is an evidence of the contract between purchaser and supplier.

4. Receiving and inspecting materials: Another important function of the purchasing department is to receive and inspect the material. In big concerns there may be a separate receiving and inspection department. But in small concerns receipt and inspection of the goods may be the duty of one person. After the materials have been received, they should be inspected by an official having technical knowledge. Whoever is the person responsible, he should get the cases opened under his supervision. Each case should contain the packing slip or delivery note. Any shortage or breakage should be intimated to the supplier. Materials received should also be tested for quality. Samples are subjected to laboratory test and results are intimated to the higher authorities. After the goods have been inspected and tested, the goods receiving clerk enters the particulars of the goods in a Goods Received Note.

5. Verifying and passing suppliers invoices: Another function of the purchasing department is to receive the suppliers bills. The bills are forwarded to the stores accounting in all respects, the stores accounting section for the purpose of verification. Having verified the bills in all respects, the stores accounting section certifies and passes the bills for payment.

3.10. PURCHASING REQUISITION

Purchase requisition is a form which is used as a formal request to the purchasing department to order goods. Purchase requisition is a document which authorizes the purchasing department to purchase goods. The purchasing department places all orders for materials and supplies in accordance with the requisitions received from:

(a) The storekeeper for all standard materials.

(b) The production control department for all special materials.

(c) The plant engineer for materials required for capital expenditure or special maintenance projects.

(d) The head of the departments requiring special indirect material.

Generally purchase requisitions are made in triplicate. The original copy will be sent to the purchasing department, one copy will be sent to the production control department and one copy will be retained in the department for reference.

The purchase requisition contains the requisition number, date, department, code number, description and quantity of material required, signature of the person initiating the requisition and signature of one or more executives approving the purchase requisition.

3.11. PURCHASE ORDER

The purchase order is a request made by the purchaser to the supplier to deliver certain goods of requisite quality and quantity at the terms and conditions agreed upon. Once the purchase order is sent to the supplier, it make payment. Thus, the purchase order is an evidence of the contract between purchaser and supplier.

Contents of purchase order: The purchase order contains the following in formations.

1. Name and address of the supplier.
2. Full description of the material and quantity.
3. Name of the buying concern, serial number and date of the order.
4. Date and place of delivery.
5. Price, discount and terms of payment.
6. Packing and dispatching instructions.
7. Signature of the authorized official.

The purchase order will be made in five copies. One copy will be sent to the supplier, one to the receiving department, one to the accounting department, one to the department which initiated purchase requisition and the last one is retained in the purchase department for reference.

3.12. BILL OF MATERIALS

Bill of material is a complete schedule of parts and materials required for a particular job or works order. Bill of material is prepared and issued by drawing office together with necessary instructions and drawings. There will be separate bill of materials for each individual kind of work. For regular products printed forms of bill of materials may be kept in stock. The bill of material serves the purpose of a purchase requisition to the purchaser, material requisition to the store-keeper and works order to the production department.

Advantages of bill of materials: This has utility to various departments as under.

1. Purchase department: It serves the purpose of a purchase requisition to the purchase department. The purchase department can immediately place orders for quantities to be purchased.

2. *Stores:* The Bill of Materials serves the purpose of a material requisition to the storekeeper. It is an authority for issue of materials.

3. *Production department:* Much time would be lost to prepare detailed material requisitions. The use of bill of material saves time and energy. Easy drawal of materials is facilitated as preparation of separate requisitions is not necessary.

4. *Accounting department:* Bill of material facilitates essay accounting of materials consumed. Costing of job becomes easier and speedier as it enables the calculation of direct material cost of before the completion of job.

3.13. GOODS RECEIVED NOTE

Meaning: Goods received note is a document which is prepared by the goods receiving clerk after the goods received from suppliers are inspected and tested. Sometimes it is the duty of the storekeeper to receive goods, in which case he will prepare the goods received note. The goods received note is the authentic record of the receipt of goods by storekeeper. Goods received note provides a complete record of all materials received. It informs the storekeeper about the quality of goods received.

This document is prepared in quadruplicate. One copy is sent to the supplier, one to the stores accounting section, one to the purchasing department and the last one is retained in the stores for their records.

The goods received notes contain the following information:

(a) Serial number and date
(b) Supplier's name and address
(c) Description, code and quantity received
(d) Order number, invoice number and date
(e) Inspection reports of goods received
(f) Bin number or stores ledger number

3.14. STORE KEEPING

Store keeping is the function which involves proper keeping of stocks, identifying and classifying them according to their nature, type and size and proper maintenance of stock records. Since material is one of the important elements of cost, it is essential that materials should be properly safeguarded and accounted for in a good stores organisation.

The stores department should be under the control of one person known as Storekeeper. He should be a man of wide experience in stores routine. He should be able to organize the operation of stress. He must be capable of controlling men under his control.

3.15. DUTIES AND RESPONSIBILITIES OF STOREKEEPER

The following are the duties and responsibilities of storekeeper:

1. The storekeeper has to accept materials or goods as ordered accompanied by goods received note. He has to place the articles in appropriate bin or shelf and has to make necessary entries on the receipt column of the bin card.
2. He has to issue materials against a properly written authority. He must not issue materials unless a properly authorized material requisition is presented. On issue he should sign the requisition slip and has to make entry on the issue column of the bin card.
3. He has to accept the materials returned from jobs or processes accompanied by Material Return Note.
4. He has to check actual physical stocks now and then and compare the figures with book figures in order to see that no mistakes or thefts have occurred.
5. He has to see that the damage to the goods while they are under his charge is minimum. He has to maintain stocks of materials in a good condition.
6. He has to report on obsolete stock, waste and scrap materials.

7. He has to watch the levels of stock, on hand and replenish stores when necessary.
8. He has to maintain the stores in a tidy manner.
9. He should not allow unauthorized person into the stirs.

3.16. TYPES OF STORES ORGANIZATION

In large manufacturing concerns, the problem often arises as to the type of organization that should be followed in the stores department. The type of stores organization depends on the class and quality of materials to be stored and nature of the business. There are three types of stores organizations which are as follows:

1. Central stores: It is the stores organisation in which buying and handling of stores is centralized. Centralized stores is always advisable from the point of view of control and economy.

Advantages: The following are the advantages of purely centralized stores:

(a) Economy in staff, floor space, records and stationery.
(b) Centralized control and better supervision is possible.
(c) Better layout of stores.
(d) The amount of capital invested in stock is minimized.
(e) Stocks are kept to a minimum, thus reducing storage space.
(f) Possibility of bulk buying at lower cost.
(g) Inventory checks and inventory control facilitated.

Disadvantages: The following are the disadvantages of centralized stores:

(a) Increased transportation costs.
(b) Inconvenience and delay in delivering goods to departments from central stores.
(c) Production stoppages in departments due to breakdowns in transport.
(d) Greater risk of loss by fire.

2. Central stores with sub-stores: In this type of stores organisation buying is centralized but handling of stores is undertaken the sub-storekeeper. Where it is disadvantageous to maintain central stores, sub-stores can be maintained.

***Advantages*:** The following are the advantages of sub-stores:

(a) It permits stocking of specialized materials for particular departments.

(b) There will be closer liason between the storekeeper and the department he serves.

(c) It avoids delay in drawing stores.

***Disadvantages*:** The following are the disadvantages:

(a) Centralized control is not possible in this type of organisation.

(b) It requires more space.

(c) The cost of storage may be increased due to increase in staff of stores.

3. Independent stores situated in various departments: In this type of stores organisation buying and handling of stores is undertaken by the buyer and storekeeper in each department.

3.17. BIN CARD

Bin card is a card which is maintained by the storekeeper for each item of stores. The bin card is purely a quantitative for each item of stores. The bin card is purely a quantitative record of receipts, issue and stores on hand. An entry will be made at the time of each receipt or issue and a new balance will be extend. It is the responsibility of the storekeeper for the correct maintenance of the bin cards. The storekeeper is answerable for any difference between physical stock and the stock balance shown in the bin card.

Bin card contains the information about description of material bin number, material code, location code, maximum level, minimum level, ordering level, etc. It will have three columns for receipt, issue and balance.

Advantages: The following are the advantages of bin cards:

(a) Bin card enable storekeeper to ascertain at a glance the quantity of any material in stock.

(b) Bin cards remind him to place purchase requisition for further supplies when the ordering level has been reached.

(c) Bin cards provide an independent check on the stores ledger.

3.18. MATERIAL RETURN NOTE

Where materials are issued in excess of requirement, the excess quantity is returned to the stores together with a material return note. Material return note is also sometimes referred to as a Stores Debit Note. The material return notes may be drawn up in the same form as a material requisition but printed in different colours to distinguish them. Material return notes are made out in triplicate, two copies are sent to the storekeeper along with the returned material. One of these is returned to the foreman with the storekeeper's acknowledgement. The copy retained by the storekeeper is entered by him on the bin cards and then passed on to the stores accountant.

3.19. STORES LEDGER

The stores ledger is a very important ledger. It is an important record in material control system forming a part and parcel of perpetual inventory system. It is written up by a stores accountant or stores clerk. It is maintained on the loose leaf or card system. It contains an accounts for each class of material. The stores ledger is thus a stock record showing receipts, issues and the balance both in quantity and value.

Stores ledger is maintained in the cost office and not in the stores. It contains the information about the name of the material, code, bin card number, maximum quantity, minimum quantity and ordering quantity. It will have columns for receipt, issue and balance. The entries in the stores ledger are made in the same way as in bin cards. The debit side is entered on the basis of Goods

Received Notes or invoices and Stores Debit Notes. The credit side is entered on the basis of materials requisitions.

Advantages: The following are the advantages of the stores ledger:

1. The future production can be planned on the basis of the information available from stores ledger without unnecessary reference to a number of books.
2. It facilitates pricing of material issues.
3. It provides a continuous record of materials received issued and discloses the balance in hand at any time both in quantity and value.

3.20. INVENTORY CONTROL

Inventory means stock of raw materials, components work in progress and finished products. Inventory control is a system of controlling inventory which ensures the smooth sailing of the production process. A good system of inventory control confirms the supply of the right quantity and quality. It ensures that the production process is not interrupted due to short supply and unforeseen demands of customers are met.

3.21. STOCK LEVELS

(a) Reorder Level

The reorder level is that level of stock at which the storekeeper initiates the purchase requisition for replenishing the stock. This level is fixed between the maximum and minimum levels. It is fixed after considering the rate of consumption, minimum level, delivery time and variation in delivery time.

Reorder level = Maximum consumption × Maximum reorder period

(b) Minimum Level

This is the minimum quantity of material which must be maintained in hand at all times. This is essentially a safely stock and hence it is not normally touched. When a particular item of material falls below this level, production is disrupted.

Minimum Level = Reordering level – (Average consumption × Average reorder period)

(c) Maximum Level

This represents the maximum quantity of materials which can be maintained in hand at all times. If stock exceeds this limit there is overstocking which leads to unnecessary blocking up of working capital. It is the sum total of minimum quantity and economic order quantity.

Maximum Level = Reorder level + Reorder quantity, – (Minimum consumption × Minimum reorder period)

(d) Danger Level

When the stock level falls below the minimum level we can say that it is a case of danger level. When the stock reaches this level the purchase officer should make special arrangement for getting fresh supplies of stock so that production is not stopped.

Danger level = Average consumption × Maximum reorder period for emergency purchases

(e) Average Stock Level

Average stock level is the average of minimum and maximum levels. It is calculated by using the following formula.

$$\text{Average stock level} = \frac{\text{Minimum level} + \text{Maximum level}}{2}$$

Average stock level = Minimum level + ½ of Reorder quantity

3.22. ECONOMIC ORDERING QUANTITY

When the stock of a particular item of material reaches the reorder level steps should be taken to get fresh supplies. But there is the question of how much to order at one time. It depends on the ordering costs and carrying cost of materials if purchases of materials are made in bulk then carrying cost will be high. On the other hand, if the size of the order is small then ordering cost is high. So an economic ordering quantity is the one which minimizes, both carrying cost and ordering cost.

The formula for calculating economic ordering quantity is

$$\text{E.O.Q.} = \sqrt{\frac{2AO}{C}}$$

where A = annual usage in units
O = ordering cost per order
C = Carrying cost percentage × cost of one unit

3.23. ABC ANALYSIS

ABC analysis is otherwise known as Always Better Control method. It is a system of inventory control which is based on selective inventory management. It exercises discriminatory control over different items of stores classified on the basis of investment involved. As such, items are divided into three categories according to their importance viz. A, B and C. 'A' category of items consist only a small percentage (say 10%) but they require a heavy investment (say 70%) of inventory valued. 'B' category of items are relatively less important. Their investment and percentage of items are more or less equal. 'C' category items do not require heavy investment but they are nearly 70% of the total items handled in stores. 'A' items require the greatest degree of control, and 'C' items the least. Between these two falls 'B' items. Hence, they are called ABC analysis.

Advantages

(a) The cost of placing orders, receiving goods and maintaining stock is minimized.
(b) Management time is saved.
(c) Much of the work connected with purchases can be systematized.
(d) Provides working capital.

3.24. CONTINUOUS STOCK-TAKING

Stock-taking or verification of physical inventory is an essential feature of every sound system of material control. The stock-taking may be either periodical or continuous. Continuous stock-taking is a system under which a selected number of stock items are verified every day or at frequent intervals throughout the year. Under annual stock-taking, stocks are verified at the end of financial year.

Annual stocking has certain disadvantages. They are as follows:

1. It causes dislocation of production departments are to be closed down during the period of annual stock-taking.
2. The element of surprise which is very essential for effective control is completely absent in annual stock taking.
3. Stock discrepancies are not detected till the end of the period. So reasons for discrepancies cannot be investigated because of lapse of time.
4. It is difficult to secure adequate trained staff to conduct annual stock-taking.

The above disadvantages can be removed by introducing continuous stock-taking.

Procedure: Under continuous stock-taking 15 to 20 items of stock are taken up every day by rotation and the physical stock is compared with the balance shown by the bin card or stores ledger. If there is disagreement, it is explained there and then. In this way all items are checked three or four times a year instead of only once under the annual stocking. Continuous stock-taking is, in fact, an essential feature of the perpetual inventory system.

3.25. PERPETUAL INVENTORY SYSTEM

Perpetual inventory system is an important aid to material control. It consists of maintaining a record for each type of material showing the quantities and value of materials received, issued and in stock. It may also contain information relating to the quantity of materials ordered from time to time, expected delivery dates and unit costs. The Institutes of Cost and Management Accountant, London, defines the perpetual inventory as "a system of records maintained by the controlling department, which reflects the physical movement of stocks and their current balance". So perpetual inventory system implies continuous maintenance of stock records. In its broad sense it covers both continuous stock-taking as well as up-to-date recording of stores books. Continuous stock-taking is, in fact, an essential feature of the perpetual inventory system.

Perpetual Inventory Procedure

Under this system a small number of stock verifiers are permanently employed. They are absolutely independent of the stores. They visit the stores daily or at frequent intervals and check a limited number of items of their choice. The items are so selected for verification that every item is checked at least once in a year. The actual quantity of disagreement, it will be adjusted in records so that the book figures agree with the physical stocks. Thus, there will continuous stock-taking.

Advantages of perpetual inventory: The following are the advantages of perpetual inventory:

1. A detailed and reliable check over the store is continuously exercised.
2. Experienced men can be employed to check the stock at regular intervals.
3. Over-stocking and under-stocking can be avoided.
4. It avoids dislocation of production which arises when stocks are checked at one time.
5. It makes the storekeeper go round his stores and observe any leakage, wastage or pilferage that might be occurring, so that such losses can be promptly checked.
6. Errors and irregularities are easily located and rectified. This gives an opportunity for preventing a recurrence in many cases.
7. As the work is carried out systematically under this system, the figures are generally reliable.
8. A system of internal check remains in operation all the time.
9. It is possible to prepare monthly or quarterly profit and loss statements and balance sheet without physical inventory being taken for all the times.

10. Due to continuous checking, the system is a kind of moral check on the staff and serves as a deterrent to dishonesty.
11. Stores records are kept up-to-date as stock-taking is carried out continuously.
12. The management is constantly kept informed of the stores position.

Disadvantages

1. The system is expensive and a small concern cannot have it.
2. The information about actual stock of a particular item on a particular day may not be available. Only book figures are available.

3.26. DISTINGUISH BETWEEN BIN CARD AND STORES LEDGER

Bin Card	Stores Ledger
1. Kept attached to bin in stores.	1. Maintained in cost office.
2. Gives information in physical units.	2. Provides information both in units as well as in rupee values.
3. Entries are made by stores clerks.	3. Entries are made by cost clerk.
4. Entries are passed on the basis of actual quantity received or issued.	4. Entries are supported by "Goods Received Note", "Material Requisition", etc.
5. Transactions may be entered in summary, periodically.	5. Transactions may be entered in summary, periodically.
6. Inter-departmental transactions do not appear.	6. Material transfers between two departments or jobs are recorded for costing purpose.
7. Normally posted when transaction is taking place.	7. Always posted long after the transaction has taken place.

3.27. PRICING OF MATERIAL ISSUES

Cost price of an article is significantly affected by the price at which materials are issued from the stores. Materials are frequently purchased at varying price and are issued to different production departments according to their needs. Frequent changes in the material prices, inflationary trends, nature of material and its storage and the frequency with which materials are issued to production departments are some of the matters which further complicate the pricing of material issues.

The following points should be considered:

1. As far as possible the method of pricing material issues should reflect the market price of the material.
2. The method should be simple and should not involve much adjustments at the closing period.
3. Frequency of receipt and issue transaction be taken into account.
4. The nature of materials and type of costing system be considered.
5. Frequent change in pricing material issues should, as far as possible, be avoided.
6. Cost of clerical work involved, as far as possible, should be minimum.
7. The proportion which raw materials bears to total cost.
8. The uniformity, if any, to be maintained within an industry.
9. The issue price should recover the purchase cost of the material. Different methods of pricing material issues.

1. Cost Price Methods

(i) The actual cost/specific price.
(ii) First-in, first-out (FIFO) price.
(iii) Last-in, first-out (LIFO) price.
(iv) Base stock price.
(v) Highest-in, first-out price.

(vi) Next-in, first-out (NIFO) price.
(vii) First-in, last-out (FILO) price.

2. Average Cost Price Methods

(i) Simple average price.
(ii) Weighted simple average price.
(iii) Periodic simple average price.
(iv) Periodic weighted average price.
(v) Moving simple average price.
(vi) Moving weighted average price.

3. National Price Methods

(i) Standard price.
(ii) Inflated price.
(iii) Replacement price.

I. First-in First-out Method or 'FIFO' Method

Under this method materials received first are issued first. In other words, materials purchased are issued at actual cost in strict chronological order. This method is most suitable in times of falling prices:

Example:

Received on 1st January 50 units at Rs. 10/- per unit
Received on 5th January 60 units at Rs. 12/- per unit
Issued on 7th January 70 units
Under this method, the 70 units are charged at

50 Units at Rs. 10/- per unit = Rs. 500
20 Units at Rs. 12/- per unit = Rs. 240
Total Rs. 740

Advantages

1. Under this method the price is based on actual cost and not an approximation. Therefore, no profits or losses arise by adopting this method.
2. This method is very useful when prices are falling.

3. This method is simple to understand and easy to operate.
4. Under this method the price of materials issued is exactly the same as paid. Hence, the cost of a product or job can be accurately known.
5. Closing stock of materials will be valued at the market price.

Disadvantages

1. Under this method clerical labour may be excessive, because whenever an issue is made the clerk will have to go through his record to find out what price is to be charged.
2. The costs of similar jobs may differ if the price changes suddenly. This renders comparison between one job and another very difficult.

II. Last-in First-out or 'LIFO' Method

Under this method the issues are priced on the assumption that the materials received an are issued first. In other words, the price of the latest consignment is used. This method is suitable in times of rising prices.

In the example given above, under this method 60 units will be costed at Rs. 12/- per unit or Rs. 720/- and 10 units will be costed at Rs. 10/- per unit or Rs. 100/- or Rs. 820/- in all.

Advantages

1. This method also ensures that materials are issued at actual cost. Therefore, neither profit nor loss is made by using this method.
2. Production is charged at the most recent prices. Therefore, it enables to fix prices on competitive basis.
3. In times of rising prices this method has the advantage of showing a lower profit, which may help in saving tax to some extent.

Disadvantages

1. This method also involves tedious clerical work.
2. Comparison among similar jobs is very difficult.

3. The stock in hand is valued at a price which does not reflect current market price. As a result closing stock will be understated or overstated in the Balance Sheet.

III. Simple Average Price

This is the price which is calculated by dividing the total of the prices paid for the material by the number of prices used in the calculation. Therefore, under this method materials are not charged out at actual cost.

For example:

On 1st August 20 units are received at Rs. 10/- per unit

On 10th August 30 units are received at Rs. 15/- per unit

On 14th August 40 units are issued.

The cost of 40 units will be: $\frac{10+15}{2}$ = Rs. 12.50 per unit

40 × Rs. 12.50 = Rs. 500/-.

Advantages

1. It is very easy to calculate.
2. When the prices of purchase do not fluctuate very much, this method is satisfactorily applied.

Disadvantages

1. This is a crude method. It produces unsatisfactory results.
2. As the materials are not charged out at actual cost, a profit or loss on material will arise.
3. Every time a fresh purchase is made, a new average price is calculated by dividing the total cost of material in stock by the total quantity of material in hand. The method average prices after weighting by their quantities. The average price at any time is simply the balance value figure divided by balance units figure.

IV. Weighted Average Price

Weighted average prices calculated by dividing the total cost of material in stock by the total quantity of material in hand. The method average prices after weighting by their quantities.

The average price at any time is simply the balance value figure divided by balance units figure.

In the above example, the cost of 40 units will be

20 units × Rs. 10/- = Rs. 200

30 units × Rs. 15/- = Rs. 450

Total Rs. 650

Rs. 650/50 = Rs. 13/- per unit

40 × Rs. 13/- = Rs. 520/-.

Advantages

1. The basis of the price calculation is very simple.
2. This method is advantageous where the prices vary widely as it cuts fluctuations of prices.

Disadvantages

1. This method is more complicated the simple average because it takes into consideration the total quantities and total cost.
2. A profit or loss in issue may be incurred as in simple average price.

V. Market Price

This method is also known as replacement cost method. Under this method the cost of the materials in hand is not considered. When an issue is made the market price is ascertained and the issue is priced at that price. In other words, issues are priced at the current market value.

Advantages

1. It discloses efficiency or inefficiency in buying.
2. This is the best method for such undertakings where quotations have to be made. Because it reflects the latest competitive condition.

Disadvantages

1. It unnecessarily complicates the costing books.
2. This method introduces an element of profit or loss in the cost itself.

VI. Fixed Price

Under this method the issue price is fixed for a whole period. The rate is used for pricing the issues irrespective of the purchase price. The main disadvantage of this method is it will introduce an element of profit or loss in the value of materials used.

VII. Standard Price

Firms which follow standard costing will use this method for pricing the material issues. Standard price is predetermined price and it is fixed on the basis each material is fixed and the actual price paid is compared with the standard price. In case the actual price is more or less than the standard price, the difference is charged to an account known as Price Variance Account. This method is easy to operate because all issues of materials are calculated at the same price.

VIII. Inflated Price

Where materials are subject to natural wastage, the cost may be inflated to account for the wages. This price includes not only the cost involved in bringing material to purchaser's premises, but also the losses arising out of evaporation, etc. Thus, if 100 units of material are purchased for Rs. 150/- and if out of this, only 90 units can be normally used, the issues may be costed not at,

Rs. 1.50 per unit but at Rs. 1.67 per unit, i.e : $\frac{150}{90}$.

Conclusion: It is considered that the weighted average price gives the best results in a majority of cases. All other methods suffer from some weakness or the other. Weighted average price evens out the widely varying prices of different adopted irrespective of whether the material is fast or slow moving and whether market price is stable or fluctuating.

3.28. SCRAP, SPOILAGE, DEFECTIVES AND ITS TREATMENT

1. Scrap

Scrap is the incidental residue from certain types of manufacture. It is a material loss. It is usually of small amount and low value. Examples of scraps are saw-dust and shortlength from wood working operations, metal from stamping operations. Scrap may be either sold or re-used.

Treatment of Scrap

1. The value realized from the sale of scrap is credited to profit and loss account like other income. This method is simple and suitable when the scrap value is negligible. This method is known as treatment by neglect.
2. From the value realized from the sale of scrap, selling and distribution costs are deducted and the net value is deducted from material cost or factory overhead. The effect of this method is to reduce material cost or overhead recovery.
3. The value realized from the sale of scrap is credited to particular job or process.

2. Spoilage

Spoilage represents that portion of raw material which has been damaged in course of manufacturing process and is disposed of without reprocessing. Spoilage occurs due to some defect in materials or operations.

Treatment of Spoilage

Accounting treatment for spoilage is based on the distribution between normal and abnormal spoilage.

Normal Spoilage

Normal spoilage is that which arises even under efficient operating conditions. Therefore, it is uncontrollable in the short run. Cost of normal spoilage is borne by good units of output.

Abnormal Spoilage

Abnormal spoilage is that which should not arise under efficient operating conditions. Therefore, it is controllable in the short run. Cost of abnormal spoilage is charged to Profit and Loss Account.

3. Defectives

Defectives are that portion of production which can be rectified and converted into finished product by the application of additional materials and labour. Defectives arise on account of sub-standard materials, careless inspection, poor workmanship and inadequate equipment.

Treatment of Defectives

1. If the defective production can be identified with specific job, the rectification cost is charged to specific job. If the identification not possible, the cost of rectification is charged to factory overhead.
2. If the defectives arise on account of abnormal circumstances, the rectification cost is charged to Profit and Loss Account.

4

Labour

4.1. DIRECT AND INDIRECT LABOUR COST

Direct Labour Cost

The labour cost incurred on the employees who are engaged directly in making the product, their work can be identified clearly in the process of converting the raw materials into finished product is called direct labour cost. For example, wages paid to the workers engaged in machining department, fabrication department, assembling department, etc.

Indirect Labour Cost

The indirect employees are not directly associated with the conversion process but assist in the process by way of supervision, maintenance, transportation of materials, material handling, etc. Their work benefits all the items being produced and cannot be specifically identified with the individual products. Hence, the indirect labour cost should be treated as production overhead. These costs will be accumulated and apportioned to different cost centers on equitable basis and absorbed into product cost by applying the overhead rates.

4.2. PAYROLL ACCOUNTING AND LABOUR COST ACCOUNTING

Payroll accounting is concerned with the maintenance of records for the amounts due to the employees like salaries, wages, allowances, contributions to provident fund and E.S.I., etc. and the deduction to be made from the employees earnings.

Payroll accounting requires the information relating to employees attendance, leaves, rates of pay, amounts to be deducted, etc.

Labour cost accounting is concerned with identifying the amount of labour cost to be charged to individual jobs and overhead accounts. For this purpose, information relating to the time spent on each job or process or number of units produced is obtained from the job cards, piece work tickets, etc. The idle time analysis is also necessary for labour cost accounting. The main objective of its is to record the time spent by all workers on each activity on a separate job card or time sheet and then apply the appropriate hourly rate. The labour costs are then charged to each of these activities. The job cards, time sheets, idle time cards are the important documents for analyzing production labour costs to various jobs and overhead accounts.

4.3. FEATURES OF INDIRECT LABOUR

The remuneration paid to indirect labour is termed as indirect wages. It is defined by the ICMA terminology as "wage cost other than direct wage cost". Examples of indirect labour are services of watch and ward, supervisor, inspector, foreman, cleaners, time keeping officers, storekeeper, general managers, etc. The following are the important features of indirect labour.

1. It is secondary in importance as compare to direct labour.
2. Its cost cannot be allocated but can only be apportioned.
3. It does not vary with the change in production.
4. It cannot be controlled.
5. Its cost is treated as overheads.
6. It cannot be identified with the finished product.

4.4. DISTINCTION BETWEEN DIRECT AND INDIRECT LABOUR

Direct Labour	Indirect Labour
1. It can be identified with finished product.	1. It cannot be identified with finished product.

2. The direct labour cost can be allocated to cost center or cost unit.	2. The indirect labour cost cannot be allocated but can only be apportioned.
3. It is a part of prime cost.	3. It is a part of overheads.
4. It is primary in the production process.	4. It is secondary or subsidiary to the production.
5. Direct labour cost can be easily ascertained.	5. It is somewhat difficult to ascertain indirect labour cost.
6. It varies according to change in output.	6. It remains fixed.
7. It can be controlled.	7. It cannot be easily controlled.

4.5. NEED FOR CLASSIFYING LABOUR

1. To ascertain the cost accurately in order to provide a basis for control.
2. To maintain efficiency.
3. To allocate overheads.
4. To introduce incentives.
5. To facilitate inter-firm composition.
6. To estimate the total labour cost.

4.6. TIME KEEPING

Time keeping refers to the process of recording the arrival and departure time of employees in a factory. In other words, it records the incoming and outgoing time of employees in a factory. Every factory will establish a separate time keeping department which is situated near the entrance of factory gate. The time keeping officer will be incharge of the department. His duty is to arrange for accurate time recording of all employees of the factory.

Objects of Time Keeping

(a) To calculate the wages payable to the employees.

(b) To calculate the normal working hours and overtime working hours of the employees.

(c) To meet statutory requirements.

(d) To calculate labour cost of an operation or job.

(e) To apportion overheads if they are based on number of workers or wages.

(f) To provide a basis for preparing statistical record which help in controlling labour cost.

(g) To introduce incentive system of wage payment.

(h) To ensure discipline among workers, i.e. regularity and punctuality. This information is also useful for the management in deciding matters relating to promotion, sanction of increments, termination, etc.

Methods of Time Keeping

Broadly speaking there are two methods of time keeping. These are (i) Manual method and (ii) Mechanical method.

1. Manual method: Under this method the attendance time of employees are recorded either by the time keeping officer or by employees themselves. The manual method of time keeping are as follows.

(a) Muster roll method or attendance register method: Under this method, an attendance register is maintained for recording the attendance time. This method is followed in small sized concerns. This method is more suitable for recording the attendance time of clerical staff and to her staff officers. Two separate columns are maintained corresponding the names of every employee. One column as to record the arrival time and second column for recording departure time. The attendance time can be marked by the time keeping officer by calling out the name of every employee or alternatively the attendance register may be signed by every employee.

Merits

1. It is simple to maintain attendance register.
2. It is economical when compared to other methods.

Demerits

1. The method is not suitable for medium and large sized business.
2. Where the attendance is marked by calling out the names of employees, there will be hold-ups near the factory gate.
3. Dishonest employees may mark the attendance of their absentee employee.
4. Time keeping officer may show step motherly treatment to his friends and this will defeat the purpose of time keeping.
5. It involves addition work for posting the entries into the individual working record.

(b) Token or disc method: A disc or token is a small metallic plate which bears the identification number of an employee. The disc of all employees may be arranged in a spike file or in a box. Whenever a worker enters into the factory gate, he is supposed to pick up at his token and place it on another file or box meant for this purpose. The box can be replaced at frequent intervals to know the employees may be asked to report to time keeping officers who in turn will record the late attendance time of employees. The time keeping officer will then prepare an attendance record with the help of disc and the absentees are denoted by the missing discs.

Merits

1. It is simple to operate.
2. It does not involve heavy investment.
3. It suits to a factory which employs more number of employees.

Demerits

1. The dishonest practice of inserting a disc of an absentee worker by another employee may take place.
2. It involves more clerical work to prepare an attendance record with the help of disc. Where any mistake is committed in recording attendance time on the basis of

disc and in case of any disputes between an employee and time keeping officer, disc cannot offer any proof.

3. It does not involve heavy investment.
4. It suits to a factory which employees more number of employees.

2. Mechanical method: In modern days mechanical methods of time keeping is used to save time and ensure greater accuracy. The machines record the exact time of the arrival and departure of employees. Thus, they avoid possible disputes and difference of opinions between employees and time keeping officers. Mechanical methods are used in medium and large sized industries as small sized concerns cannot afford to invest more capital on such large sized industries as small sized concerns cannot afford to invest more capital on such equipments. The following are the important mechanical methods of time recording.

(a) Dial time recorder: The features and functioning of this equipment can be summarized as under:

(i) It consists of a large dial on which there are about 150 holes corresponding to the number of workers.

(ii) A clock is fitted within the circle of the dial together with a dial arm which operates from the center of the circle.

(iii) The worker while entering into the gate turns the dial arm. He then presses the button corresponding to his clock number. The time of his arrival is recorded on a sheet of paper kept inside the machine.

(iv) The same procedure is followed before the employee leaves the factory gate.

Merits

(i) Time is recorded strictly according to payroll order.

(ii) Time of arrival and departure are separated out in two different sheets of paper which require additional clerical work.

(iii) A worker cannot see the time he has booked and disputes may arise afterwards.

(b) Card time recorder: This is a machine which is fitted with a clock on each side of which there is an "in" and "out" rack which contains the cards of the employees. The worker who enters the gate takes his card from the "in" rack, inserts it in the machine. On pressing a lever the time of arrivals is recorded on the card. Then the card is placed in the "out" rack. At the time of departure from the factory the worker removes his card, inserts it in the machine to record the time of departure and finally places it in the "in" rack.

Merits

(i) For each and every worker time is recorded individually.

(ii) The absence of worker can be checked by a mere look at the "out" rack.

(iii) This can be taken as a basis for wage calculation.

Demerits

(i) An employee can record the time of absentee worker.

(ii) Controlling and checking cards become difficult.

(c) Autograph or signature type time recorder: This type of machine is most commonly used in small sized business enterprise where supervision for time recording does not arise.

Features

(i) It is a machine which is fitted with a clock and is connected to a printing mechanism on a roll of paper.

(ii) To operate the machine, the employee opens the shutter by pressing a lever which is at the side of the machine. This enables to uncover a small signature window.

(iii) The employee signs in this signature window and as he signs, the day and time is automatically recorded.

(iv) When the lever is released, the paper roll inside the machine—which now bears worker's signature window, and the machine is ready for the signature of the next worker.

Merits

(i) Recording of time is automatic and accurate.

(ii) Employees cannot see the recorded time.

Demerits

(a) The worker's name does not appear as per the payroll order.

(b) The signature may not be legible.

(c) Breakdown in the machine leads to stoppage in the recording of attendance time.

4.7. TIME BOOKING

Time booking refers to the process of recording the time spent by workers on various jobs in a factory. In other words, it is the recording of the starting time and finishing time of employees on a job. Time booking comes next in the sequence after the time keeping in respect of recording time.

Methods of Time Booking

Time booking can be entrusted to the foreman or to time booking clerks. Sometime it is done even by employees. It can be recorded either manually or mechanically. The following are the various methods of time booking:

1. Daily time sheet system: Under this method the time spent by workers on different jobs for a certain day is recorded. For each worker a sheet of paper is issued wherein his time spent on various jobs are recorded. This method is suitable under two situations, viz. (a) size of the factory is small, and (b) where the worker has to attend to more jobs instead of few jobs on the same day. The daily time sheet consists of the following particulars:

(a) Worker's name

(b) Worker's identification number

(c) Name of the department

(d) Date of work

(e) Job number

(f) Nature of work done

(g) Starting time on the job
(h) Finishing time on the job
(i) Actual or normal hours and overtime hours of work done
(j) Signature of time booking authority.

Merits

(a) It is simple to operate.
(b) It enables the foreman to know how much the work is done by employee each day.
(c) The record shows accurate information as it is checked by the foreman everyday.
(d) This method is particularly useful where more number of jobs are to be performed on the same day.

Demerits

(a) It involves more of clerical work by way of consolidation of all the daily time sheets for one full month.
(b) It is not suitable for large business concerns.

2. Weekly time sheet: This method resembles to daily time sheet of time booking. But instead of booking the time daily, it is recorded for the week. It provides the data relating to the time spent on various jobs for a period of one week.

3. Job cards or job tickets: Under this method a card is made use of for recording the time spent by workers on various jobs instead of sheets of paper. Each employee will be given a card which contains the particulars of work to be performed by him. This card is to be filled in by employees by noting down the starting time and finishing time of the job which he attends to. When a worker completes a job he will be given a separate job card to book the time on such job.

Merits

(a) It provides information relating to the job to be performed by workers. Thus, it serves as an authority to start the work, besides recording the total time spent by workers on jobs.

(b) Reconciliation of attendance time and time booked on job becomes difficult when idle time is not properly recorded.

4. Combined time and job card: This document contains two parts is to be filled in as attendance time and the second part, the total time spent on jobs. The facilitates reconciliation of gate time with the work time and the extent of idle time can be easily detected. This method fulfills the objectives of both time keeping and time booking.

Merits

1. It combines the merits of both attendance time and time booking.
2. Compared to maintaining time keeping and time booking separately, it is more economical.
3. The idle time is properly accounted for.

Demerit

It is not suitable for large sized undertakings.

5. Labour cost card: A labour cost card is used to record the time spent by all the workers on various operations of the job. In other words, the time spent by a group of workers attending on a job is recorded in labour cost card. This card is meant for a job instead of workers. As this card shows the total labour cost of a particular job it is termed as labour cost card.

6. Piece work card: This card shows the number of units produced by the worker and the time spent in manufacturing the units. This method is adopted where piece rate system of wage payment is adopted. A separate card is prepared and used by every worker to record the number of units produced and the total time spent by him.

4.8. DISTINCTION BETWEEN TIME KEEPING AND TIME BOOKING

Time keeping	Time booking
1. It records attendance time of employees.	1. It records the total time worked by employees on jobs.
2. It is the first step involved in time recording.	2. It is the second step involved in time recording.
3. It records the time spent by employees on various jobs.	3. It records the time spent by the employees in the factory.
4. Time keeping is done at the time-keeping office.	4. It is done at various production departments.
5. It is recorded by time keeping officer.	5. It is recorded by a foreman or by employees.
6. Its purpose is to enable preparation of payroll.	6. Its aim is to ascertain the labour cost of job.

4.9. JOB EVALUATION

Job evaluation is a procedure designed to rank jobs on a formal basis and to measure the worth of a job for compensation purposes in relationship to other jobs. It requires written detailed description of work operations encompassed by each job. The descriptions are used to rate jobs according to such facts as skill, responsibility, effort and conditions. The ratings employed to group particular jobs into labour grades with associated pay brackets.

Objectives of Job Evaluation

The main objectives of job evaluation are as follows:

(a) To eliminate wage inequalities.

(b) To establish sound wage differentials among the jobs.

(c) To provide a sound wage for incentive and bonus plan.

(d) To establish a sound wage structure.

(e) To facilitate maintenance of a consistent wage policy.

Advantages of Job Evaluation

(a) Wage rates can be fixed accurately in an organisation by deciding the proper worth of the different jobs.

(b) Job evaluation technique is useful for proper selection, training, promotion, transfers of employees within the organization. These activities can be performed objectively and impartially through job evaluation.

(c) It facilitates objective control on the entire organization and eliminates nepotism and wastage.

(d) It eliminates or at least minimizes the grievances of the workers about the absolute and relative wage rates. It avoids confusion in the minds of employees as regards the wage rates fixed by the management.

(e) Job evaluation technique raises the morale of the employees and also efficiency of labour force in factories.

Methods of Job Evaluation

There are four methods of job evaluation. They are as follows:

1. Ranking method: This method is also known as the grading method as it involves assigning grades to various jobs in the order of their relative importance. Under this method, three steps are involved, viz. (a) making a thorough job analysis, (b) expressing the findings of this analysis in job description, and (c) ranking each job by arranging them in an ascending order, starting with the job of minimum requirements of various characteristics and ending with maximum requirements of various characteristics of the job. Ranking can be based on: (i) difficulty of work, (ii) volume of work, (iii) responsibility involved, (iv) supervision required, (v) knowledge, and (vi) conditions under which work is done.

After ranking is completed, the jobs are generally grouped into ten or twelve groups, according to their position. The jobs are then evaluated by determining the wage rates prevailing in similar factories. Accordingly, wage rates are increased either by a fixed percentage or by a fixed amount.

2. Job classification method: Under this method, standard grade description is used in classifying the various jobs. As and when each job is reviewed, it is placed in the category having the most appropriate description. This quite opposite of what happens in the job ranking system, since in that system, jobs are first ranked and then divided into grades.

3. Points methods: This method is by far the most widely used method in factories. It consists of a yardstick containing various factors such as skill, education, responsibility and so on that are inherent in the jobs. The degree of importance of each factor is determined by an arbitrary decision, and a suitable point value is specified for each factor. The total points for all the factors then determine the relative position of that job among other jobs.

4. Factor comparison method: This method consists of analyzing jobs on the basis of five factors, viz. mental requirements, skill requirements, physical requirements, responsibility involved and working conditions. The jobs are ranked according to each one of these factors, one factor being taken at a time and each job is compared with the other with respect of its worth on this factor alone. The relative weightage of this factor on each job is done by applying money value (i.e. rupees) to the ranking. After all the jobs are rated on each factor, a wage rate for each job is determined by the sum of money weightage determined for each of the five job factors. These wage rates become the basis for determining the wage scale.

4.10. MERIT RATING

Merit rating is concerned with the evaluation of individual employee. It is a technique used to rate an employee's performance to assist in determining whether a person should receive a merit award, promotion, demotion, etc. In merit rating an individual worker's certain characteristics like attendance, co-operation, discipline, acceptance of responsibility, integrity, honesty, intelligence, skill, etc. are assessed to measure the worth of individual worker.

Objectives of Merit Rating

Merit rating serves the following purposes:

(a) It furnishes a periodic record of the relative value of each employee, as judged by his superior.

(b) It determines and justifies wage differentials existing for the same job.

(c) It provides a more accurate information on which promotions, transfers, and lay-offs may be based.

(d) It provides a means of evaluating the selection and training techniques used.

(e) It provides information for counselling employees, so that the means of overcoming weakness can be pointed out and programmes for self-improvement developed.

(f) It provides a more effective tool for rating the personnel.

(g) It establishes better employer-employees relations through mutual confidence, which comes as a result of frank discussions between the leader and the follower regarding merit rating.

(h) It ensures better supervision as the supervisors must observe the employees closely if they are to rate them accurately.

4.11. STUDIES AT WORK PLACE

(i) Time study: It refers to the analysis and determination of the time necessary to perform a given task. It replaces the old practice of using past performance, judgement, or trial as a method of establishing the time allowed for the performance of a task. Time study has been defined by Alford and Beathy as a scientific analysis of methods and equipments used or planned in doing a piece of work, development in practical detail the best way of doing it, and determination of the time required.

(ii) Utility of time study: The management makers use off time study for the following purposes:

(a) To determine the standard time for the peformance of an operation and use the data for establishing a fair incentive system of wage payment.

(b) To estimate the time and cost involved in new production orders.

(c) To achieve a uniform flow of work in developing or improving the layout of a plant.

(d) To aid the analysis of work methods conducted during motion studies.

4.12. MOTION STUDY

Motion study has been defined by F.B. Gilberth as "the science of eliminating. Wastefulness resulting from using unnecessary, ill directed and inefficient motions". Motion study consists of dividing work into the most fundamental elements possible, studying these elements separately and in relation to one another and from these elements, the unnecessary movement of workers organ's are eliminated.

A micro-motion study is the sub-division of an operation into motions and their analysis for the improvement of the work cycle. Detailed bodily movements, especially highly skilled motions are recorded and the time is measured by taking motion pictures at a constant speed with a micrometer from the background.

Advantages of Motion Study

(a) By simplifying the movements and reducing the sequence, it enables the worker to produce more units per hour and earn more wages. The employer is also benefited by the increased production.

(b) It helps in carefully planning material handing equipments which not only increases speed of production but also reduces material handing cost.

(c) It helps the foreman to know the causes for the slow progress of work and enables him to train the workers the best method of performing the task.

(d) It helps the personnel department to induct the right type of workers into the jobs for which they are best suited.

(e) It leads to better safety measures.

4.13. WORK STUDY

Work study, in its broadest sense, is the application of systematic analysis to the work of men and machines so as to improve methods and to establish proper time values for that work. The objectives of work study are:

(a) The most effective use of plant.

(b) The most effective use of human effort.

(c) A reasonable work load for those employed.

Work study investigates every aspect of existing or proposed work in order to find the best way of performing tasks. It involves setting standards and solving problems which include bottlenecks, low morale, large amounts of defective work and low productivity. Work study is comprised of methods study and work measurement. Work study is a general term for those techniques (especially method study and work measurement) that are used in the examination of human work, and which lead systematically to the investigation of all factors affecting the efficiency of the situation being reviewed as a basis for making improvements.

4.14. REMUNERATION METHODS

The labour remuneration methods, plans and systems are broadly classified into three categories as given below:

(i) Time rate methods; (ii) Piece rate methods; and (iii) Group bonus plans.

(I) Time Rate Method

In time based wage payment system standard time is pre-determined and the efficiency of each individual worker is assessed to compensate them for higher efficiency in work as compared to standard time set.

1. Flat time rate method: Under this system the worker is paid on hourly, daily or weekly wage rate and his remuneration is based on the time spent for production and wages are calculated as follows:

$$\text{Wages} = \text{Hours worked} \times \text{Hourly wage rate}$$

2. High day rate system: Under this method, employees are paid a high hourly wage rate than the rate paid at different organizations in the industry or region expecting that the workers will work more efficiently. To implement this method, the efficient, skilled and experienced workers are selected expecting and efficient and hard work from them in expectation of that the organization will pay wages at higher rates than prevailing in the industry.

3. Halsey premium bonus plan: Under this method, for each unit or job a standard time is calculated and 50% of the time saved is allowed as bonus. The time rate paid for the time taken plus 50% of the time saved, it the job is completed in less than the standard time, and time rate is guaranteed. The total wages of a worker is calculated as follows:

$$\text{Total wages} = (\text{Time taken} \times \text{Hourly rate}) + \left[\frac{50}{100} \times \text{Time saved} \times \text{Hourly rate}\right]$$

4. Rowan premium bonus plan: Under this method, a standard time is calculated for every job or process and a bonus is paid upon the time saved calculated as a proportion of the time taken which the time saved bears to the time allowed. In contrast of Halsey Plan, instead of fixed percentage of time saved, bonus is in the proportion of time saved to time allowed. Under Rowan plan, the total wages are calculated as follows:

$$\text{Total wages} = [\text{Time taken} \times \text{Hourly rate}] + \left\{\frac{\text{Standard time} - \text{Time taken}}{\text{Standard time}} \times \text{RPH}\right\}$$

Comparison of Halsey and Rowan Plan

- Where the worker completes his work within half the time allowed; the bonus under both the plans will be same.
- It time saved is less than 50% of time allowed, the Rowan plan is beneficial for the worker.

5. Halsey-Wair plan: This is a modified system of Halsey premium bonus plan. This is also called as $33\frac{1}{3} - 66\frac{2}{3}\%$ sharing plan. According to this plan, $33\frac{1}{3}$ % of the time saved will be paid to the worker as bonus and the remaining $66\frac{2}{3}$ % is shared by the employer.

Total wages = (Time taken × Hourly rate) +

$$\left[33\frac{1}{3} \times \text{Time saved} \times \text{Hourly rate}\right] 100$$

6. Emerson's efficiency bonus plan: This plan is also called as Emerson's empirical plan. It provides for guaranteed time wages to the worker and the bonus is paid according to the efficiency of the worker. The formula for calculation of earnings of worker is given below:

Efficiency

1. Below $66\frac{2}{3}$ % efficiency
2. $66\frac{2}{3}$ % to 100% efficiency
3. Over 100% efficiency

Percentage of Bonus

Time wages. No Bonus.

A bonus increasing from 0.01% to 20% above basic wages on 100% efficiency.

A bonus of 20% above basic wages plus 1% increase in efficiency.

Emerson used 32 different steps. The step bonus rates are as follows:

Efficiency	Bonus
67-75%	1%
76-85%	4%
87%	7.56%
90-95%	10%
96-100%	20%

Under Emerson's plan, 100% efficiency is considered as standard. The efficiency percentage is calculated as follows:

(i) If time is considered:

$$\text{Efficiency} = \frac{\text{Standard time}}{\text{Time taken}} \times 100$$

(ii) If output is considered:

$$\text{Efficiency} = \frac{\text{Actual output}}{\text{Standard output}} \times 100$$

7. Barth variable bonus plan: This plan is also called as variable sharing plan. Under this system the earnings of a worker is calculated by multiplying the hourly rate of pay with square root of the product of standard time and time taken.

$$\text{Earnings} = \text{Hourly rate} \times \sqrt{\text{Standard time} \times \text{Actual time}}$$

This plan is difficult to understand by the workers and hence it is not popular. This plan may specially be used for trainees, beginners, apprentices and unskilled workers. The main disadvantage of this plan is that total wages is higher for less efficient people. As the efficiency increases, the earnings of a worker decrease. This plan discourages the efficient workers.

8. Bedaux Points Plan: Under this system, the standard time is fixed for completion of the job and each minute of time is called Bedaux point. Time wages are paid up to 100% efficiency and bonus is paid on the basis of number of Bedaux points saved. A worker gets a bonus which is equal to 75% of Bedaux points saved and 25% is either retained by the employer or paid to foremen and indirect workers. Under this plan timer wages are guaranteed.

Formula:

Wages = Time taken × Hourly rate

Bonus = 75/100 × Bedaux points saved × Point rate

9. Gnatt's task bonus plan: This system is a combination of both time and piece wage systems. Day wages are guaranteed under this plan. Standard time is set for a job or task and the worker's efficiency is ascertained by comparing the actual performance with the standard set.

Formula:

Output

1. Output below standard
2. Output at standard
3. Output above standard

Payment

Time rate, i.e. guaranteed day wages.

120% of time rate, i.e. time rate + 20% of time rate as bonus.

120% of piece rate, i.e. high piece rate.

(II) Piece Rate Method

Under piece rate systems of wage payment, the worker's efficiency is measured in terms of production against standards set. A worker who produces more units than standard set for him is eligible for bonus in piece rate wage payment systems.

Merits

- Employee morale is more due to higher earnings.
- Increased production result in decrease in cost of production per unit.
- It is possible to set accurate labour standards.
- A task is done in the most economical manner which reduces labour cost.
- Less supervision is required resulting less cost of supervision.
- Productivity of the organization will increase.

- Labour cost can be accurately estimated.
- Optimum utilization of resources is possible.

Demerits

- Quality may deteriorate in order to increase the production quantity to earn more.
- Safety conditions may be violated by the workers in order to increase production which may lead to accidents at work place.
- There may be apprehensions regarding rate cutting.
- Unskilled workers sometimes earn more than skilled workers if the latter have to work on time basis.
- If rates are not uniform for same type of jobs, it causes discontent among workers.
- It involves more calculations and detailed production records are to be maintained.
- The worker's health may be affected due to over-strain taken by the workers to earn more wages.
- Inefficient workers may envy the efficient ones which may cause unrest.

(a) **Straight piece rate method**: Under this method, a fixed wages rate is paid for each unit of production, job completed or number of operations completed irrespective of the time spent on it. The wages are calculated as follows:

This method is used where the production is repetitive in nature and it cannot be applied to the work which requires skill and artistic work. The workers' pay depends upon his output and not upon the time he spends in the factory. The supervision cost is reduced as workers are paid depending on their actual units produced. This method will act as an incentive to efficient workers and act as disincentive to inefficient workers.

The main disadvantage is that the production may need to be thoroughly inspected for its quality. The stoppage of work due to abnormal causes like machine breakdown, failure, shortage of power, etc. may cause the workers to loss their wages, and they feel insecure under this method of wage payment. The spoilage, defectives and wastage of materials is more, if this wage plan is adopted, due to reckless use to achieve higher output.

(b) Piece rate with guaranteed time rate method: Under this method, the employee is assured of agreed level of wages for the specified level of performance. The wage rate consists of two components. The first component is of fixed nature depending on the time spent the wage are paid and the other part is variable in nature linked to merit rating and cost of living. The main disadvantage in this method is that it is more complicated in computation of wages and it is not popular.

(c) Differential piece rate method: Under this method, an incentive is offered to workers to increase their output by paying higher rates for increased levels of production.

Under the straight piece rate system, the time factor is not taken into consideration but under differential piece rate plan, a series of production targets will be established and as each target is reached a new piece work rate will apply.

In this plan the fast doing skilled workers can able to reach higher levels of targets and will be compensated at higher piece rates. The extra rates of pay can act as in inducement to the employee to aim for higher productivity to increase their earnings by putting more efforts. Differential piece work plan is normally accompanied by the guaranteed day rates.

(d) Taylor's differential piece rate system: In this system the inefficient workers are penalized by paying him low piece rate and rewarding the efficient worker by paying him a high piece rate for the higher production. Minimum wages are not guaranteed under this method.

Formula:

(i) 80% of normal piece rate when below standard (low piece rate).

(ii) 120% of normal piece rate when at or above standard. (high piece rate).

This method penalizes not only those workers that are not only below the standard but even those whose output is just below the standard output.

(e) **Merrick's differential piece rate system:** It is also called as Merrick's multiple piece rate system. Under this system three piece rates are used unlike the Taylor's differential piece rate system which consists of only two piece rates. This system is an improvement of the Taylor's system by eliminating its disadvantages.

Formula:

Efficiency	Piece rate applicable
1. Up to 83 %	Normal piece rate
2. Above 83 % to 100%	110% of normal piece rate
3. Above 100%	120% of normal piece rate

(III) Group Bonus Plans

In time rate methods and piece rate methods, the efficiency of each individual worker is considered for wages and bonus calculations. But under group bonus plans, different groups of workers are identified and the task is given to the group and the efficiency of the whole group, instead of each individual worker, is determined for computation of bonus and earnings. The bonus is distributed among the workers belonging to the particular group on pre-determined basis.

The group incentive plans can be successfully implemented where:

- Output depends on team work and joint efforts of group of workers.
- It is difficult to measure the individual result rather than the group's result.
- It is necessary to work as a member of a team rather than on individual basis, for example, in chemical process industry, an individual worker cannot influence the production of the plant.
- Both direct and indirect workers need to be compensated equally.
- It is possible to create small work units/groups to set the standards to production and costs.

- Skill of the workers in the group does not vary widely.

Advantages

- Increase in production and saving in cost of production can be achieved.
- Supervision costs will be reduced substantially.
- The quality of work is improved.
- Absenteeism is reduced to minimum and creates interest in work among the workers.
- It creates team spirit and collective interest in the work.
- Minimises waste and reduces cost per unit.
- Clerical work in calculation of bonus is reduced.

Disadvantages

- Individual skills and efficiency are not considered in these systems.
- Difficulty may arise in calculation of bonus and method of its distribution to all the workers in the group.
- The bonus is paid on group efforts, an individual worker may not put his maximum effort in view of equal sharing of bonus by inefficient workers.
- An inefficient group leader may cause the entire group to suffer.

4.15. CO-PARTNERSHIP

Co-partnership schemes also known as co-ownership involve the issue of shares to employees so that they may feel identified with the business. The employees being shareholders also will take more care of machines and materials as it will increase the sense of belonging and will work towards the progress of the organisation along with that their share value also increases. The improved productivity means low cost of production and higher profits, and improved standard of living of the workers.

Advantages

- It helps to reduces labour turnover.

- Contribution of employees to the profitability of the concern is recognized.
- The morale of the employees is high.
- The employees will have a greater since of belonging since they also hold share capital in the organization.

Disadvantages

- The lack of production-oriented incentive system will not create any interest in work.
- Political interference may also possible due to employees association in managements.
- Efforts and rewards are not properly related.
- It does not differentiate between efficient and inefficient workers.
- Even though employees are admitted into partnership they will not have any voice in management decision-making.

4.16. REQUISITES OF GOOD WAGE INCENTIVE PLAN

For design and introduction of good wage incentive plan the following points are considered:

- It should be simple to understand by the workers and should enable themselves to calculate their earnings.
- It should be simple to administer and reduce clerical work.
- It should be capable of using computers for increase in speed of calculations.
- It should be introduced only after full consultation and agreement with the workers and unions.
- It should act as a motivational scheme.
- It should guarantee the minimum day wages.
- It should be ensured to operate for a long period.
- It should cover as many employees as possible.
- The incentive should be paid as quickly as possible after the completion of the work.

- The cost of administration of the scheme should be minimum.
- The incentives should relate to the efforts and efficiency of the workers.
- The abnormal factors should be paid only on good production units and discouragement for defective work.
- The incentives should be paid only on good production units and discouragement for defective work.
- The standards of work should be set after scientific study of work and the performance levels should be fair to reach.
- It should conform to labour laws and regulations of the land.
- It should minimize labour turnover and absenteeism.
- No limits should be placed on additional earnings under the scheme.
- It should be at least equivalent to the incentive schemes prevailing in other units or industries in the region.
- Due consideration should be given for the saving in cost of production due to the incentive plan and the incentive that will pass to the workers.

4.17. LABOUR TURNOVER

Whenever employees in a factory get better terms and conditions of employment elsewhere, they leave the existing factory and join the new factory. This change in labour force is known as labour turnover. Thus, labour turnover refers to mobility of employees from factory to factory for getting better opportunities in terms of earnings and position of anthority. In concrete terms, labour turnover may be defined as the number of employees who leave the factory during a period in relation to the average number of workers employed during the year.

Although a minimum labour turnover is quite normal and can be allowed in factories, excessive rate of labour turnover is not desirable. This is because efficient and experienced workers leave the factory and new employees come and occupy their places. Naturally, the ability of such new workers is less as compared to that of the experienced workers. The desirable percentage of labour turnover is placed between 3 per cent and 5 per cent.

(I) Causes of Labour Turnover

The causes of labour turnover may be listed under the following headings:

1. Causes arising from the point of view of employees

(a) Incompetence to perform a job satisfactorily.
(b) Insubordination to superiors.
(c) Accidents.
(d) Prolonged illness.
(e) Death.
(f) Marriage in case of women employees
(g) Housing problem.
(h) Discharge on disciplinary ground.
(i) Retirement.
(j) Personal betterment.

2. Causes arising from the point of view of employers

(a) Payment of low wages.
(b) Bad working conditions.
(c) Failure to protect workers against accidents.
(d) Hostile attitude on the part of superior towards subordinates.
(e) Unfair promotion policies.
(f) Inefficient management.
(g) Lack of welfare facilities.
(h) Lack of job security, social security and training facilities.

(II) Effects of Labour Turnover on Cost of Production

1. Increased wages due to less speed in production.

2. Additional expenses incurred on training the newly recruited employees.
3. Increased cost of labour arising out of rectifying the spoilt and defective products.
4. Increased idle time wages as new workers are always less efficient.
5. Overhead expenses will increase cost per unit owing to lower volume of production.
6. Cost of repairs and maintenance will increase.
7. Payment of higher compensation to employees involved in industrial accidents.

(III) Remedial Measures to Prevent High Labour Turnover

The following measures are to be taken to control and reduce the high percentage of labour turnover:

1. Scientific recruitment, selection and training of workers.
2. Provision of better wages, allowances and other monetary benefits.
3. Provision of better working conditions.
4. Introduction of fair promotion policy.
5. Provision of social security measures such as pension, provident fund, gratuity and so on.
6. Better motivation and provision of welfare facilities to employees.
7. Cordial labour management relations.
8. Reducing fluctuations in the volume of work.
9. Ensuring job satisfaction and job security.
10. Measures should be taken to reduce labour disputes to the minimum.

(IV) Measurement of Labour Turnover

Labour turnover can be measured by any one of the following three methods. In this connection it is to remember that once a particular method is adopted, it should not be changed frequently as comparison of labour turnover becomes difficult.

1. Separation method: This is the most commonly used method of measuring labour turnover. Under this method, the total number of separations during a period is divided by the average number of workers on roll during that period and multiplying the quotient by 100 to determine the percentage of turnover. The average number of workers during a period is obtained by adding the number of workers in the beginning and at the end of the year and dividing the sum by 2. Expressed in the form of formula:

$$\text{Separation method} = \frac{\text{No. of separation during the period}}{\text{Average no. of employees during the period}} \times 100$$

2. Replacement method: This method takes into consideration only the actual replacement of labour, i.e. the number required to be replaced during the period, irrespective of total leavings. This is obtained by dividing the number of replacement during the period by the average number of employees during that period and then multiplying it by 100 to determine the percentage. Expressed in the form of formula:

$$\text{Replacement method} = \frac{\text{No. of replacements during the period}}{\text{Average no. of employees during the period}} \times 100$$

3. Flux rate method: This method takes into account both the leaving and the new entrants. This is obtained by adding the leavings and replacements, dividing the total by the average number of employees during the period and multiplying the quotient by 100. Expressed in the form of a formula:

$$\text{Flux rate method} = \frac{\text{No. of separation + no. of replacements}}{\text{Average no. of employees during the period}} \times 100$$

(V) Treatment of Labour Turnover Cost

Labour turnover cost can be classified into (i) preventive cost and (ii) replacement cost. Preventive cost includes all expenses incurred in preventing excess labour turnover. Such costs relate to providing welfare facukutues. Replacement cost includes cost spent on new workers employed in place of workers who leave the factory. Such as recruitment cost, training cost, cost of defectives and so on. Labour cost is not treated as direct cost. Hence, they are accumulated over a period of time under the above two classifications and are charged to various departments as overheads on the basis of number of workers in each department.

4.18. CASUAL WORKERS

A casual worker is a worker who is appointed on a temporary basis on a daily wage basis in order to meet the increased production schedule. Casual workers can also be appointed to replace workers who would have met with industrial accidents. As and when casual workers are appointed a separate accounting is to maintain for such workers. They should be under the care of supervisor and their output must be certified by the supervisor.

The wages payable to the casual workers are to be treated as direct wages and as such it is charged directly to the job on which casual workers have been worked.

4.19. OUT WORKERS

Out workers are engaged to work outside the premises of employees. Out workers may be classified under two categories viz.: (i) those who work with their own tools in their own houses, and (ii) those who are sent to the premises of customers by the employers. No record need be maintained in respect of first category of employees. However, control is to be exercised over them with regard to issue of materials, prompt production of good and quality of finished goods. For the second category of workers, it is necessary to maintain records for the purpose of recording attendance time and time spent on the jobs.

4.20. IDLE TIME

In the production process, lost time may occur for several reasons. The idle time is the difference between hours paid and hours worked. Where the workers are paid on time basis, the idle time is the difference between the time for which the workers were paid and that which they actually spent of production process. It is the labour time paid for but not utilized in production. The idle time is classified into two types: (i) normal idle time and (ii) abnormal idle time.

Causes of Idle Time

Causes of Normal Idle Time

A part of idle time is unavoidable and is considered as a normal occurrence in the factory. Illustrative list is given below:

- Travelling time from one job or department to another.
- The distance covered between the factory gate and the department or actual place of work.
- Elapse of time between finishing one job and starting another job.
- Time spent to overcome fatigue.
- Tea and lunch breaks.
- Machine or job setting up time, etc.

Causes of Abnormal Idle Time

The important causes for the abnormal time are given below:

- Temporary lack of work
- Machine breakdown
- Power failures
- Shortage of raw materials
- Waiting for tools
- Waiting for jobs due to unplanned production
- Stoppage of work due to managerial policy decisions

- Strikes and lockouts
- Floods, earthquakes, etc.

4.21. OVERTIME PREMIUM

Overtime premium is paid to the workers for the extra time worked than the normal working hours specified in the Factories Act, 1948 or work agreement with the union. The extra time is paid at a higher rate than the normal time rate. For example, if a worker works beyond 8 hours in a day or 48 hours in a week, he is paid with double the wages for the extra time worked. The overtime wages consist of two elements: (i) normal wages for extra time and (ii) additional wages paid for the overtime worked.

Accounting Treatment of Overtime Premium

- Overtime hours at the normal rate are treated as direct labour cost and charged to production on the same basis as time worked during normal hours but the premium paid during the overtime periods not a direct charge against production but is recovered as production overhead through overhead recovery rate.
- Where the overtime is worked on a specific job to meet the time schedules or to carry out specific rush orders for which extra price is recovered, then the entire labour cost can be charged as direct labour to that job.
- If overtime wages paid due to negligence or delay of worker of a particular department, it may be charged to the concerned department.
- If the overtime premium is paid due to abnormal causes, it should be charged to Costing Profit and Loss Account.

5

Overheads

5.1. DEFINITION OF OVERHEAD

Overheads are the indirect costs which cannot be allocated to any specific job, or process because they are not capable of being identified with any specific job process. Overheads include cost of indirect material, indirect labour, indirect expenses which cannot be conveniently charged to any job, process cost unit, etc. For example, costs like rent, rates, administration and supervision, depreciation, maintenance, selling and distribution expenses, cleaning materials, etc. cannot be directly attributed to cost units produced the costing treatment of overheads deals with methods whereby these indirect expenses can be related to cost units.

CIMA defines Overhead Cost as "the total cost of indirect materials, indirect labour, and indirect expenses". Overhead is the cost of materials labour and expenses which cannot be economically identified with specific saleable cost unit.

5.2. CLASSIFICATION OF OVERHEADS

Classification of costs refers to the process of grouping costs according to their common characteristics. Overhead costs may be grouped according to

1. Functions,
2. Elements, and
3. Behavior.

1. Function-wise Classification

It refers to the classification of overhead costs with reference to the various major activity divisions of a concern. The main groups of overhead on the basis of functions are:

(a) Factory overhead;

(b) Office and administration overhead;

(c) Selling overhead; and

(d) Distribution overhead.

(a) Factory overhead: Factory overhead refers to all expenses other than direct material costs, direct wages and direct expenses incurred in a factory in connection with manufacturing operations. Examples of factory overhead are—rent of factory building, municipal taxes and insurance of factory building, depreciation of factory building, depreciation and insurance of factory plant and machinery, repairs and maintenance of factory buildings and machinery, salary of factory manager and other factory staff, factory power and lighting, cost of small tools, consumable stores, lubricating oil, cotton waste, salary of store-keeper, expenses of store keeping, fuel, gas, water, drawing office salaries, factory stationery, cost of idle time, overtime wages (if not treated as direct cost), telephone charges of factory, cost of training of new workers, labour welfare expenses, etc.

(b) Administration overhead: Administration overhead refers to all expenses relating to the direction, control and administration (not connected directly with production, sales or distribution) of an undertaking. Examples of administration overhead are: general management salaries, salaries of general office staff, office rent, depreciation of office building, rates and insurance of office building, office lighting and air-conditioning, depreciation of office furniture and office machinery, repairs and maintenance of office building, office furniture and office machinery, audit fees, legal charges, office stationery, telephone charges of office, bank charges, directors' fees counting office salaries, etc.

(c) Selling overhead: Selling overhead refers to all costs of seeking to create and stimulate demand or of securing orders. Examples of selling overhead are: sales office expenses, advertisements, salary of sales manager, salaries of other selling staff, commission on sales, traveling expenses, expenses of traveling agents, cost of price lists, catalogues and samples, bad debts, rent of showroom, depreciation of showroom, rates and insurance of showroom, lighting and cleaning of showroom, expenses of branch establishments, expenses of sales and publicity department, cost of training to salesmen, postal expenses relating to sales, legal expenses for recovery of bad debts, cost of entertainment of customers, market research expenses, cost of preparation of tenders, etc.

(d) Distribution overhead: Distribution overhead refers to all expenses incurred from the time the product is finished in the factory till its delivery to ultimate customers or consumers. Examples of distribution overhead are: rent of warehouse, insurance, rates and lighting of warehouse, depreciation running and maintenance of delivery vans, salaries of van men, carriage on sales, packing charges, cost of after-sales service, salary of warehouse-keeper, and the like.

2. Element-wise Classification

It refers to the classification of overhead with reference to the various elements on which costs are incurred. The main groups of overhead on the basis of elements are:

(a) Indirect material costs,

(b) Indirect wages, and

(c) Indirect expenses.

(a) Indirect material costs: Material costs which cannot be allocated but which are to be apportioned to or absorbed by cost centers or cost units, are known as 'Indirect Material Costs'. Examples of indirect material costs are: consumable stores, cotton on waste, small tools, lubrication oil, coal, fuel, etc.

(b) Indirect wages: Indirect wages refer to the labour cost or wages which cannot be allocated but which are to be apportioned to or absorbed by cost centers or cost units. Examples of indirect wages are: salary of foreman, salaries of supervisory staff, salary of factory manger, salary of timekeeper, salary of storekeeper, idle time wages, leave pay, etc.

(c) **Indirect expenses:** Indirect expenses refer to expenses (other than indirect material costs and indirect wages) which cannot be allocated but which can be apportioned to or absorbed by cost centers or cost units. Examples of indirect expenses are: factory rent and rates, depreciation of factory building, insurance of factory building, depreciation of plant and machinery, factory, repairs and maintenance, etc.

3. Behaviour-wise Classification

By 'behaviour', we mean the reaction of the expenditure for changes in the volume of output. Some overhead costs increase with the increase in the volume of output, some remain constant irrespective of the changes in the level of output, whereas some others do not vary upto a certain volume but vary after that. The main groups on the basis of behaviour or variability are:

(a) Fixed overhead;

(b) Variable overhead; and

(c) Semi-variable or semi-fixed overhead

(a) Fixed overhead: Fixed overhead refers to expenses which tend to remain constant or unaffected (in aggregate) by changes in the volume of output. For example, if the monthly salary of the Works Manager is Rs. 2,000 and the monthly output is 10,000 units and in a particular month the production falls down to 8,000 units, we cannot make a corresponding cut in the works manager's salary. The monthly expenditure of Rs. 2,000 thus remains constant and is not affected by the fall in output. Similarly when the output increases, there is no increase in the monthly salary of the works manager. The other examples of fixed overhead are: rates and taxes on building, insurance of building, factory rent, supervisor's salary, etc.

Fixed overhead costs are not always wholly fixed in nature. This is because over a long period of time, if the concern decides to go in for additional equipments and buildings and appoints some additional staff to cope with the increase in production, these result in a permanent change in the level of production and the fixed charges which were constant within a certain range of plant capacity do also increase now. Thus, the total fixed overhead costs remain constant only within the limits of plant capacity and any appreciable change in the latter affects the fixed overheads.

(b) Variable overhead: Variable overhead refers to expenses which tend to change (in aggregate) directly with changes in volume of output. Such expenses increase in aggregate as the output goes up and decrease proportionately when the output falls. However, there may not always be a perfect mathematical relation. The examples of variable overhead are: indirect materials, fuel and power, carriage outward, packing materials, lighting, internal transport, store losses, idle time, etc.

(c) **Semi-variable overhead:** Semi-variable or semi-fixed overhead costs refer to expenses which are partly fixed and partly variable. These costs are fixed upto a certain volume of output. If, however, the output rises beyond that limit, these costs shall increase in aggregate although the increase in the expenditure will not be proportionate to the increase in output. Examples of semi-variable overhead costs are: depreciation of plant and machinery, repairs and maintenance, costs of supervision, service department wages, postage and stationery, etc.

5.3. ADVATAGES OF CLASSIFYING OVERHEAD INTO FIXED AND VARIABLE

The necessity for the classification of overhead into fixed and variable elements arises due to the following reasons:

1. Effective Cost Control

Better control over expenses can be exercised if a proper classification of overhead into fixed and variable elements has been made. Fixed expenses are incurred by management decision and as such can be controlled by the top management while variable expenses can be controlled by lower management.

2. Helpful in Decision-making

The classification of expenses into fixed and variable elements is of immense help to the management in making a number of business decisions, such as make or buy decision, selection of suitable sales mix, operate or shut-down decision, expansion or contraction of the production of various products, etc.

3. Fixation of Selling Price

This distinction is very helpful in determining the selling price of the products or services. Sometimes, a manufacturer charges different prices for the same article in different markets to meet varying degrees of competition. However, the lowest selling price of any product should atleast cover prime cost plus variable overhead. This classification also helps in determining the price during trade depression or in a special market.

4. Marginal Costing and Cost-Volume Analysis

The classification of overhead into fixed and variable elements is very essential for the technique of marginal costing and break-even analysis. It helps in ascertaining marginal cost, i.e. the total variable cost attributable to one unit of output. Further, it assists in determining the break-even point, i.e. the volume of output where there is no profit and no loss.

5. Helpful in Budgetary Control

This classification is very helpful in the preparation of flexible budgets. A flexible budget is a budget which is designed to change in accordance with the level of activity actually attained. Flexible budget for various levels of activity can be prepared with the help of this classification.

6. Absorption of Overhead

This classification helps in the proper absorption of the different items of overhead. The method to be adopted for determining the absorption rates depends on the nature overhead.

But the usefulness of this classification suffers from a number of limitations. First in classifying the overhead into fixed and variable factors other than volume such as product specification, product mix, price indices, conditions of efficiency, plant an variable costs is not always true. Further, the analysis of overhead into fixed and variable elements depends mainly upon historical costs which, in their own turn, suffer from number of limitations.

5.4. STEPS IN OVERHEAD ACCOUNTING

(I) Codification of Overheads

Codification of overhead is a system of assigning code number to each head, sub-head and category of expense to facilitate the systemic and easy recording, accounting, summarization of cost data for ascertainment of cost, profitability and managerial decision-making.

CIMA defines a coding as "a system of symbols designed to be applied to a classified set of items, to give a brief accurate reference facilitating entry, collation and analysis".

The importance of coding is vital with the mechanized and computerized systems of costing. A good coding system should consist of clear, unambiguous and distinctive codes in order to systematise the analysis of overhead for accurate cost ascertainment expeditiously and with least cost.

The distinction between standing order number and cost account number is that standing order numbers are applied to production overhead expenses by custom, whereas cost account numbers are applied to administration, selling and distribution, research and development costs. The compilation method is similar in both the methods.

Objectives of Codification

The important objectives of codification is given below:

- For apportionment of similar items of expenses on one suitable basis of apportionment.
- It systematizes the recording and accounting of cost data and control of expenses.
- The computerized cost accounting is made easier with codification of accounts.
- It will reduce the clerical work in organisation with huge number of accounts.

- It facilitates automatic allocation, apportionment and absorption of overheads to different cost units or cost centers.

Methods of Codification

The following methods are used in codification of overheads:

(a) **Straight numbering method:** Under this system each item of expenditure is allotted a fixed number. This method is also called numerical coding system. For example:

Factory rent	-	21
Office rent	-	22
Sales office rent	-	23 etc.

Number blocks: Under this method each head of expenditure is given one block of numbers. This method is slight variation of straight numbering system.

Depreciation	-	1 to 100
Insurance	-	101 to 200
Repairs and maintenance	-	201 to 300

The block of numbers allotted will depend on the sub-heads to be accommodated.

(b) **Memoric method:** Under this method alphabets are used as codes to help the memory. For example:

Depreciation-Office Buildings	-	DOB
Depreciation-Factory Buildings	-	DFB
Depreciation-Godown	-	DG

(c) **Decimal method:** Under this method, numerical codes are allotted to various expenses and cost centers classifying into major, minor and detail account heads given below explain the method of codification under decimal method.

1. Production Overhead
    1.1. Indirect Materials
        1.1.1. Consumable Store
        1.1.2. Cotton Waste

1.1.3. Lubricants
1.1.4. Loose Tools
1.2. Indirect Labour
1.2.1. Time Office
1.2.2. Security
1.2.3. Clerical Staff
1.3. Indirect Expenses
1.3.1. Factory Rent
1.3.2. Depreciation of Plant and Machinery
1.3.3. Insurance of Factory Building
2. Administration Overhead
2.1. Indirect Materials
2.2. Indirect Labour
2.3. Indirect Expenses

(d) **Field method with numerical codes:** Under this system each code number consists of nine digits as the first two digits represent the variable or fixed nature of expense, the next three digits indicate head of expense, the next two digits stand for the analysis of expense and the last two digits indicate the cost center, where expenses have been incurred. For example, code 10/100/03/05/ represents for:

Fixed/Production Labour/Monthly Salary/Machine Shop.

(e) **Combination of symbol and numbers:** Under this method, a combination of symbol alphabet and a number is used to represent a code. For example:

I1 - Insurance Factory Building
I2 - Insurance Administrative Building
I3 - Insurance Plant and Machinery
I4 - Insurance Vehicles, etc.

Here alphabet represents the main head of the expense and number represents the analysis of expense.

(II) Departmentalisation of Overhead

Departmentalisation of overhead is the process of determining the departments or operations according to which the expenses are to be apportioned. In other words, departmentalisation of overhead refers to the allocation and apportionment of overheads to production and service departments. After overhead costs have been collected under various standing order numbers, the next step is to allocate and apportion them to production and service departments. This process of departmentalisation of overhead is also known as 'Primary Distribution of Overhead'. Departmentalisation of overhead involves two steps namely:

(a) Allocation of overhead.

(b) Apportionment of overhead.

Allocation of Overhead

'Allocation' has been defined by the Institute of Cost and Management Accountants, London as "the allotment of whole items of cost to cost centers or cost units". Allocation of overhead is the function of identifying overhead items with particular cost centers or production and service departments. Overhead costs arising solely from the existence of a particular department (production as well as service department) can be charged or allocated to that department. Generally the salary of departmental head, foreman's salary and the cost of indirect materials issued to a particular department are allocated to that department.

Apportionment of Overhead

'Apportionment' has been defined by the Institute of Cost and Management Accountants, London as "the allotment of proportions of cost to cost centers or cost units". Apportionment of overhead is the process of distributing those items of overhead which cannot be allocated to a cost center or department, between cost centers or departments on an equitable basis. Overhead costs such as factory rent, factory insurance, factory require apportionment to different production and service departments on some equitable or reasonable basis.

(III) Overhead Distribution Summary

It refers to a statement or summary prepared on periodical basis, in order to show the allocation and apportionment of overhead costs to production and service departments of the factory. The overhead distribution is also known as 'Primary Distribution Summary'.

(IV) Principles of Apportionment of Overhead

Selection of a suitable base for the apportionment of overhead to production and service departments is an important aspect of overhead accounting. For this purpose, the following principles may serve as guide.

1. Service or Utility

This is the most important principle of apportionment of overhead and is based on the theory that a department should be burdened with the overhead in proportion to the benefit derived or service utilized by that department on account of overhead. For example, the rent or depreciation of the building may be apportioned on the basis of area occupied by each department in the building. This principle is very consistent and fair but requires the maintenance of detailed records of various facts and figures.

2. Analysis or Survey

Sometimes, it may not be possible to ascertain the extent of the benefit derived by various departments on account of overhead. In such a case, an analysis or survey of the expenses with reference to their impact on different departments may be made. For example, the salary of the works manager has to be apportioned on the basis of time devoted by him to different departments.

3. Ability to Pay

This principle lays down that the share of overhead apportioned to each department depends upon the ability of the department to bear it. The department making higher profits should be made to bear a higher burden of expenditure. The principle does not take into account the actual cost conditions which render it inequitable.

4. Efficiency

This principle is of recent origin. Under this approach, production targets are fixed for each department and overhead costs are apportioned with reference to these targets. If a department fails to achieve the targets, its unit cost goes up, indicating its efficiency in the form of reduction in unit cost. Thus, under this approach, a type of incentive is introduced as every department head aspires to achieve or exceed the fixed target.

(V) Bases for Apportionment of Overhead

As regards the basis to be used for apportioning the overhead cost, there is no hard and fast rule. Further, no single basis can be applied to apportion all items of overhead. The basis to use for apportionment shall be determined with reference to the nature of the particular item of overhead. Some of the common bases for apportionment of overhead may be given as follows:

1. Floor Area or Floor Space

Some of the items of overhead are apportioned on the basis of the floor area occupied by various departments. Such expenses include rent, rates and insurance of building, lighting, etc.

2. Direct Wages

Under this basis, the items of overhead costs are apportioned in proportion to the direct wages of the departments. This base is used for those items which are related to direct wages, e.g. contribution to Provident Fund, contribution to Employees State Insurance Scheme, etc.,

3. Number of Workers

Under this basis, the overhead costs are apportioned in the ratio of number of workers engaged in each department. This basis is adopted where the expenditure depends on the number of workers in various departments. Salary of the supervisory staff is apportioned on this basis.

4. Direct Labour Hours

Under this basis, the overhead costs are apportioned in proportion to the number of labour hours worked in various departments. Salary of the supervisory staff is apportioned on this basis.

5. Number of Machine Hours

This basis is used for the purpose of apportionment of overhead costs to departments where machines are more dominant factor than men.

6. Value of Assets

In respect of the expenses relating to capital assets, the values of various assets are used as the basis for apportionment, e.g. depreciation, insurance, repairs and maintenance of plant and machinery.

7. Lighting points

The electricity charges of the manufacturing concern are apportioned on the basis of the number of lighting points.

8. Kilowatt Hours

This basis is adopted for the apportionment of cost of electric power.

9. Technical Estimates

In cases where a conventional basis for apportionment of overhead costs cannot be used, equitable proportion can be estimated by experts on the basis of technical assessment. This basis can be used for steam cost, internal transport, etc.

5.5. RE-APPORTIONMENT OF SERVICE DEPARTMENT EXPENSES TO PRODUCTION DEPARTMENTS

After the apportionment of the overhead costs to production and service departments, the next step is to apportion the total expenses of various service departments to production departments. Since the service departments are not engaged in actual output, it becomes necessary to apportion the costs of the service departments to the production departments. The process of re-apportionment of service department costs to production departments is also known as 'Secondary Distribution'.

Bases of Re-apportionment

The service department costs are apportioned to the production departments generally on the basis of the benefits derived by the production departments from the service department. Following is the list of the more conventional bases used for the apportionment of service department costs:

Basis of Apportionment

Time-keeping Department, Wages office

Number of workers, labour hours worked, machine hours worked.

Personnel Department.

Number of employees in each department.

Purchase Department.

Number of purchase orders placed, cost of materials purchased.

Stores Department.

Number of material requisitions. Value of materials used.

Maintenace Department.

Number of labour hours worked machine hours worked.

Building Service Department.

Floor space occupied.

Canteen Department, Welfare Department, Recreation, Ambulance Service.

Number of employees in each department.

Internal Transport Department.

Weight or value of materials handled.

5.6. METHOD OF RE-APPORTIONMENT

There are two methods in use for the apportionment of service department costs which are as follow:

1. Apportionment of service department costs only to production departments.
2. Apportionment of the service department costs to the production as well as other service departments.

1. Apportionment of production departments only: Under the first method, service department costs are directly apportioned to the production departments and the service rendered to the other service departments is ignored.

2. Apportionment of production departments and other service departments: This method applied for apportioning the service department costs, considers inter-service department distribution on some equitable basis. Inter-service distribution can be done by the following methods:

(a) Step ladder method: Under this method, all service departments of a concern are arranged in the order of their utility in terms of their service to the largest number of other departments. Thereafter, the cost of the most serviceable department, i.e. the department which serves the largest number of departments, is first apportioned to other service departments and production departments. The service department which serves the next largest number of departments is then taken up and so on in this order till the costs of all the service departments are apportioned. The cost of the last service department will naturally be apportioned only to the production departments. Under this method, the shape of the apportionment chart looks like the shape of ladder and as such it is known as steps ladder method.

(b) Repeated distribution method: Under this method, the service department costs are repeatedly distributed to other departments (production as well as service) on some equitable basis or on the basis of agreed percentages till the figures of the service departments are exhausted or become negligible.

(c) Simultaneous equation method: Under this method, the actual costs of service departments are obtained first by solving simultaneous equations. The costs so obtained are then transferred to production departments on the basis of agreed percentages.

(d) Trial and error method: Under this method, first of all the cost of the first service department is apportioned to other service departments in the given ratio. Then the cost of the next service department is apportioned to the first and other service departments. This process goes on till the service department costs are exhausted or become negligible.

5.7. ABSORPTION OF OVERHEAD

After the overheads have been allocated and apportioned to various production departments, the total overhead cost of a production departments shall comprise of:

(i) the expenses allocated to the production department, e.g. salary of the departmental head, salary of departmental foreman, cost of indirect materials issued to the department, etc.

(ii) the share of the common expenses apportioned to it, e.g. factory rent, salary of works manager, factory power, factory lighting, etc.

(iii) the share of the expenses of the service departments re-apportioned to it, e.g. expenses of personnel department, expenses of the stores department, expenses of time-keeping department, etc.

The total amount of overhead accumulated for a production department is ultimately to be charged to the various cost units of that department. The distribution of the accumulated overhead cost of a production department amongst its cost units is known as overhead absorption. Overhead absorption is defined as the allotment of overhead to cost units. Thus, absorption of overhead is the function of apportioning overhead costs to individual units, jobs, production lots, processes, work-orders or such other convenient cost units and is also known as 'recovery' or 'application' of overhead expenses to cost units.

5.8. METHODS OF FACTORY OVERHEAD ABSORPTION

1. Units of Output Method

Under this method, absorption of factory overhead is made on the basis of the number of units manufactured. The overhead rate is obtained by dividing the amount of overhead expenses by the number of units of output, thus:

$$\text{Overhead rate} = \frac{\text{Factor overhead of the department}}{\text{Number of units of output}}$$

This method is a very simple and direct method of overhead absorption and can be applied in single output industries like collieries, brick-making, etc. where only one product or a few grades of the same product are manufactured. But this method cannot be applied in multi-product industries where variety of products of different values are manufactured.

2. Direct Material Cost Method (Percentage on Direct Material Cost)

Under this method, the absorption of overhead is made on the basis of direct materials consumed. The overhead rate is expressed as a percentage of the direct material cost and is calculated by dividing the factory overhead for a particular period by the cost of direct materials used during the period and multiplying it by 100. Thus, overhead rate is:

$$\text{Overhead rate} = \frac{\text{Factory overhead}}{\text{Cost of direct materials used}} \times 100$$

This method is very simple and equitable where the same type of material is used in the articles manufactured and the price of such material is not subject to consider fluctuations.

3. Direct Labour Cost Method (Percentage on Direct Wages)

Under this method, the absorption of overhead is made on the basis of the direct wages. The overhead rate is expressed as a percentage of direct wages and is obtained by dividing the factory overhead for a particular period by the direct wages paid during that period as multiplying it by 100. The overhead rate is obtained by applying the following formula:

$$\text{Overhead rate} = \frac{\text{Factory overhead}}{\text{Direct wages}} \times 100$$

This method is very simple and is widely practiced on account of the following advantages:

(a) Automatic consideration is given to the time factor as the wages are paid on the basis of time.

(b) Wages rates are more constant than material prices and hence this method provides a stable basis for the absorption of overhead.

(c) Factory expenses, to a great extent, depend on the number of workers employed and hence this basis is more equitable.

4. Prime Cost Method (Percentage on Prime Cost)

Under this method, absorption of overhead is made on the basis of prime cost. This method assumes that both materials and labour give rise to overhead and therefore both should be taken into consideration. The overhead rate is expressed as a percentage of the prime cost and can be obtained by the following formula:

$$\text{Overhead rate} = \frac{\text{Factory overhead}}{\text{Prime cost}} \times 100$$

This method is simple to operate and combines the advantages of both direct materials cost and direct labour cost methods. But this method assigns equal weight to materials and labour, though factory overhead is more closely related to labour.

5. Direct Labour Hour Rate Method

Under this method, absorption of overhead is made on the basis of number of hours for which direct labour is employed. The direct labour hour rate of overhead is obtained by dividing the factory overhead for the department for a given period by the total number of direct labour hours for the period. Thus, overhead rate is:

$$\text{Overhead rate} = \frac{\text{Factory overhead}}{\text{Number of direct labour hours}} \times 100$$

6. Machine Hour Rate Method

Under this method, overhead absorption is made on the basis of the cost of operating a machinery. This method is applied in highly organized engineering works where most of the work is done by machines. The hourly cost of operating a machine represents the overhead rate and is known as machine hour rate. The machine hour rate is obtained by dividing the factory expenses connected with a machine for a given period by the number of hours worked by the machine during that period. Thus, overhead rate under the machine hour rate method is:

$$\frac{\text{Factory overhead (relating to a machine)}}{\text{Number of machine hours}}$$

In highly machanised factories where a considerable portion of the factory overhead is related to the running of the machines, machine hour rate method provides the most scientific basis for the absorption of overhead. It requires the maintenance of accurate records regarding the life of the machines and the cost of repairs and maintenance.

7. Dual Hour Rate Method

This is a combination of machine hour rate and direct labour hour rate. It is adopted in those departments where both manual and machine work are equally important. In such cases, overheads are classified into two groups, i.e. overheads which are related to manual work and secondly those related to machine work. The first kind of overheads is absorbed by means of a labour hour rate and the second category of overheads by a machine hour rate.

6

Single or Output Costing

6.1. SINGLE COSTING

This method of costing is applied to ascertain the total and per unit cost of a standard product turned out in a manufacturing concern. Output costing method (which is also known as single costing) is generally applied to industries where the following features are present:

(a) The output of production is continuous.

(b) The units of output are identical.

(c) The units of output are natural.

(d) It is desirable to ascertain the cost per unit of output, e.g. per metre, per kilogram, per ton, etc.

The above mentioned features are present in industries like collieries, brick works, flour mills, quarries, cement mills, paper mills, iron and steel mills, sugar mills, etc. which are engaged in producing only one type of product or a few grades of same product.

6.2. OBJECTIVES OF OUTPUT COSTING

The main objectives of output and single costing method are:

(i) to ascertain the total cost and per unit cost of production during a specified period;

(ii) to make comparative study of the cost of production; and

(iii) to ascertain or to determine the selling price per unit of goods manufactured.

6.3. COST SHEET

Cost sheet is a statement, prepared at given intervals of time, which provides information regarding elements of cost incurred in production. It discloses the total cost as well as the cost per unit of the product manufactured during the given period. If it is desired to compare the costing results of a particular period with any of the preceding periods, comparative columns can be provided in the Cost Sheet.

Cost Sheet vs. Statement of Cost

Some people make a distinction between 'Cost Sheet' and 'Statement of Cost', the former denoting a statement presenting cost analysis on unit basis and the latter (Statement of Cost) denoting a statement showing the total cost figures. However, both terms may be used inter-changeably.

6.4. FEATURES OF COST SHEET

The basic features of cost sheet are as follows:

(i) The statement is usually prepared under the output costing method where the object is to ascertain the per unit cost of production.

(ii) A cost sheet is prepared for a specified period of time, generally for a month, quarter, half year or year.

(iii) The cost sheet generally contains the following information:

(a) Period,

(b) Total output,

(c) Cost of raw materials consumed,

(d) Cost of direct labour,

(e) Details of chargeable expenses,

(f) Details of overheads namely factory, office and administration and selling and distribution, and

(g) Aggregate of elements of cost at various stages, e.g. prime cost, works cost, office cost and total cost.

6.5. ADVANTAGES OF COST SHEET

The following are the main advantages of cost sheet:

1. It discloses the total cost and the cost per unit of the units produced during the given period.
2. It enables the manufacturer to keep a close watch and control over the cost of production.
3. It acts as a guide to the manufacturer and helps him in formulating a define useful production policy.
4. It helps the manufacturer to minimize the cost of production when there is a cut-throat competition.
5. It helps the manufacturer by providing cost data of previous year for comparison. Such comparison helps in the detection of inefficiency and wastage.
6. It helps in fixing up the selling price more accurately.

6.6. PREPARATION OF COST SHEET

(I) Treatment of stock: Stock may be of raw materials, work-in-progress and finished goods.

(a) Stock of raw materials: Opening stock of raw materials is to be added to raw materials purchased.

Closing stock of raw materials is to be deducted from raw materials.

(b) Stock of work-in-progress: Work-in-progress at the beginning is to be added to prime cost to get works cost.

Work-in-progress at the end of the period is to be deducted from prime cost to get works cost. Work-in-progress is usually valued at works cost basis.

(c) Stock of finished goods: Opening stock of finished goods is to be added to cost of production to get cost of goods sold.

Closing stock of finished is to be deducted from cost of production to get cost of goods sold.

(II) **Scrap or waste:** The amount realized from the sale of defective materials is to be deducted from the cost of raw materials.

If units produced are found defective and are sold as scrap or wastage, the amount thus obtained should be deducted from factory expenses or from works cost.

Abnormal wastage of materials or time should not be shown in cost accounts.

6.7. TENDER OR QUOTATIONS

The business concern may be required to submit a tender, or to quote prices for the supply of the commodities it produces or for completing job. The preparation of tenders requires information regarding prime cost, works, administration and selling overheads, and profit of the preceding period. The manufacturer has to find out the possible changes in prices of material, rates of wages and other costs. He has to certain as the amount of variable, semi-variable and fixed overheads on the basis of past experience. He must have a reasonable amount of profit by taking into consideration the market conditions. In preparation of estimates or tenders, overheads are generally not given. They are estimated as percentage on wages. Similarly administration, selling and distribution overheads are estimated as percentage on work cost basis.

6.8. SPECIMEN OF COST SHEET

COST SHEET

Period..........

Output.........

Particulars	Total Cost		Cost per Unit	
	Rs.	P.	Rs.	P.
Direct materials	x x	x	x x	x
Direct Wages	x x	x	x x	x
Direct Expenses	x x	x	x x	x
Prime Cost	x x	x	x x	x

Works Overhead	x x x	x x x
Works Cost	x x x	x x x
Office and Administration Overhead	x x x	x x x
Cost of Production	x x x	x x x
Selling and Distribution Overhead	x x x	x x x
Total cost	x x x	x x x
Profit	x x x	x x x
Sales	x x x	x x x

6.9. COST SHEET VS. COST ACCOUNT

It is desirable to understand the difference between a cost sheet and a cost account. A cost sheet is a statement, prepared at given intervals of time, which provides information regarding elements of cost incurred in production. It discloses the total cost as well as the cost per unit of output and provides for the comparison of costing results of a particular period with any of the preceding periods through comparative columns. In short, it is a statement prepared on memorandum basis and does not form a part of the double entry system in cost accounts.

A cost account, on the other hand, is an account forming part and parcel of the double entry system of cost accounting which discloses the details of expenditure actually incurred upon a particular job, contract or a process. Unlike a cost sheet, a cost account deals with the result of a one operation or job and does not disclose the result of the whole operation for a given period of time.

6.10. DISTINGUISH BETWEEN COST SHEET AND COST ACCOUNT

The main distinction between the cost sheet and cost account may be summarized as follows:

1. Cost sheet is a statement showing cost of production per unit or total output. Cost account is a ledger account maintained in the Cost Ledger on the principles of double entry system.

2. Cost sheet is an independent and isolated summary of costs relating to a job or a certain volume of output. Every cost account is a part of integrated cost accounting system of the entire organization.

3. Cost sheet is prepared for a short period, say for three or six months while production continuous. Cost accounts are kept for accounting period as a whole and are prepared when the production is completed.

4. Cost sheet shows the costing data in an analytical manner to suit the purpose for which it is prepared. Cost accounts make a presentation of total amount of costs without analysis.

5. Cost sheet presents costing data on unit basis. Cost account does not depict unit cost.

6. Cost sheet is prepared for the purpose of cost determination, cost comparison, pricing, cost control and cost estimation. Cost accounts make a record of actual costs incurred for the purpose of preparing Costing Profit and Loss Account.

7

Contract Costing

7.1. MEANING OF CONTRACT COSTING

The system of cost accounting employed by builders, civil engineering contractors, constructional engineers and ship builders is known as contract costing. Contract costing is a type of job costing in which a contract constitutes a unit of cost. In principle it is similar to job costing. A separate account is maintained for each individual contract for the purpose of determining the profit made or loss incurred. The most important aspect of contract costing is that most of the costs can be allocated direct to contracts. Contract account is debited with all the items of cost and credited with the contract price. The balance represents profit or loss on the contract.

7.2. RECORDING OF COSTS OF CONTRACT

The procedure of recording costs in contract account is as follows:

1. Materials: Materials purchased directly or supplied from store will appear on the debit side of the contract account. Material returned to store is credited with contract. Materials transferred from one contract to another are recorded in the usual way. At the end of the accounting period the value of materials at site is carried forward.

2. Wages: Wages of all workers engaged on a particular contract are charged direct to that contract. Wages paid and outstanding are to be debited to contract account.

3. Expenses: All expenses other than material and direct wages are charged direct to contract as and when they are incurred.

4. Plant: Plant and tools are often required for executing a contract. When plant and tools are used in a particular contract, the depreciation may be charged in any one of the following ways:

(a) When the plant and tools are used for a long time, the total cost of plant and tools is debited to contract account in which they are used. When the contract is completed the contract account is credited with sale proceeds plant, if it is sold. If it is not sold the contract account is credited with the depreciated value.

(b) The difference between the original cost and depreciated value at the end of the period is ascertained and debited to the contract account as plant depreciation.

5. Sub-contracts: When a sub-contractor is engaged for a special work connected with the main contract, the work performed by the sub-contractor forms a direct charge to main contract. Sub-contract cost is shown on the debit side of the contract account.

6. Indirect expenses: The contractor incurs several office and administration expenses. Since they are incurred for the benefit of the whole business, they have to be allocated to different contracts on some suitable basis. The allocation can be made in proportion to (a) materials, (b) direct wages, (c) prime cost or any other suitable basis.

7.3. PROFIT ON INCOMPLETE CONTRACTS

The long-term nature of contracts has necessitated to determine profit to be attributed to each accounting period. In the long-term contracts it is considered the their outcome can be assessed with reasonable certainly before their conclusion, the attributable profit should be calculated on a prudent basis and included in the accounts for the period under review. The profit taken up should be based on standard cost accounting principles. In case of completed contracts all the profit that arises from the contract can be transferred to Profit and Loss Account. But in case of incomplete contracts, only portion of the profit is taken to the Profit and Loss Account depending on the extent of work completed on the contract because some provision is to be made for meeting contingencies and unforeseen loss. There are no hard and fast rules in calculation of profit to be taken Profit and Loss Account. But in general, the following principle are followed:

If loss is arrived on incomplete contracts, the entire loss is debited to Profit and Loss Account.

Profit should be considered only in respect of work certified. The uncertified work should be valued at cost.

If the amount of work certified is less than 25% of the contract price, then no profit should be taken to Profit and Loss Account, and the entire amount is kept as reserve for meeting contingencies.

If the amount of work certified is more than 25% but less than 50% of the contract price, then 1/3rd of profit ascertained as reduced by percentage of cash received from the contractee should be taken to the Profit and Loss Account. The balance will remain as reserve for meeting contingencies. The formula is given below:

$$\text{Notional profit} \times 1/3 \frac{\text{Cash received}}{\text{Work certified}}$$

If the amount of work certified is 50% or more of the contract price, then 2/3rd profits ascertained as reduced by percentage of cash received from the contracted is to be taken to Profit and Loss Account, keeping the remaining amount in reserve. The formula is given below:

$$\text{Notional profit} \times 2/3 \frac{\text{Cash received}}{\text{Work certified}}$$

If the contract is nearing completion, the total cost of completing the contract may be estimated if possible and then ascertain the estimated total profit. The amount of profit is transferred to the Profit and Loss Account depending upon the condition and contingencies of the concern.

The balance amount of profit not transferred to Profit and Loss Account but kept as reserve for meeting contingencies and is shown in the Balance Sheet assets side by deducting it from the amount of work-in-progress. It is carried down as a credit balance in the contract account itself, the work-in-progress being represented by the debit balance in the contract account.

7.4. SURVEYOR'S CERTIFICATE AND RETENTION MONEY

In contract works, a Surveyor or an Architect or Civil Engineer is appointed to periodically visit the site for inspection of the work completed. He will issue a certificate mentioning the stage of completion of work and the value of the work completed to the date of issue of certificate. The payments will be released to the contractor by the contractee based on the said certificate.

Normally the payments will be released only to the certain percentage, say 80% of the work certified. The balance amount of work certified is retained by the contractee till the completion of the entire contract satisfactorily. The amount so retained is called 'retention money'. The contractee so retains to safeguard himself from the risks that may arise from the contractor. Usually the percentage of retention money is upto 20% of the amount of work certified.

7.5. WORK-IN-PROGRESS

Work-in-progress means the jobs in various stages of completion at the end of the financial year. The value of work-in-progress is shown on the asset side of the Balance Sheet. The value of the work-in-progress is estimated as follows:

1. In the case of contracts which have made little progress, the total net expenditure incurred upto date is taken to be the value of work-in-progress.
2. In the case of contracts which have made appreciable progress, the value of work certified is added to the value of work uncertified and from this the profit carried forward is deducted.

7.6. DISTINGUISH BETWEEN JOB COSTING AND CONTRACT COSTING

The important distinguishing features of job costing and contract costing is given below.

Job costing	Contract costing
1. Job work is carried in the premises.	1. Contract work is carried at site.
2. An order, a unit, lot or batch of product may be taken as cost unit.	2. Each contract is a cost unit.
3. Cost is first allocated to cost centers and then charged to individual jobs. It is a system of costing in which the elements of cost are accumulated separately for each job or work undertaken by an organization.	3. Most of the expenses are of direct nature and are directly charged to respective contract accounts. Only general overheads and head office expenses are apportioned to individual contracts.
4. The prices of the jobs are fixed basing on the nature of costs and policy of the firm.	4. The pricing is generally through bidding and external forces have major influence in fixing the offer price.
5. The duration of the job work is smaller.	5. Generally the contract works will take more time to complete.
6. The value of the job work would be lesser.	6. The contract works are bigger in nature and the value of the contract would also be higher.

7.7. COST PLUS CONTRACT

Cost plus contracts provide for payment of allowable actual costs plus an agreed element to cover the profit as incentive.

Cost plus contracts will be entered mainly in the following situations:

(a) Existence of sole supplier of product or service.

(b) Product or service is highly complex in nature and the costs cannot be pre-determined.

(c) When the product or service is a new or special one for which no cost estimates are available.

(d) In a highly inflationary situation cost plus basis is more secure when the estimate based on current costs are uncertain.

(e) Cost plus contracts are more popular in government for defense equipments and components, ships, aircrafts, etc.

8

Job Costing and Batch Costing

8.1. MEANING

Job costing is the method of costing which is applied to ascertain the costs of specific jobs or work-orders which are treated as contracts of small size. These jobs as generally dissimilar of non-repetitive nature and may not be comparable with each other. This method is also known as 'Job Lot Costing' or 'Lot Costing'.

8.2. FEATURES OF JOB COSTING

The special features of job costing may be summarized as follows:

(i) Under job costing, production is carried on by a manufacturer against customer's order and not for stock.

(ii) Each job or work-order is of a separate nature.

(iii) The jobs or work-orders are generally executed in factories, work-shops and repair shops. But sometimes the job work is also done outside the factor; or work-shop, e.g. plumbering job, sewerage work, etc.

(iv) The unit of costing, under this method, is a job or specific work-order.

(v) Under this method, the production and its requirements are determined first and then the expenses are ascertained in relation to it.

8.3. SUITABILITY OF JOB COSTING

Job costing method is most suitable to such activities as printing press, painting and decorating, automobile garages, repair shops, electrical fittings, fittings, ship building engineering works, plumbering works, etc. where work is done according to the customer's specifications.

8.4. ADVANTAGES OF JOB COSTING

The main advantages of job costing can be summarized as follows:

(i) Job costing enables the manufacturer to know the profitability of each job separately.

(ii) It provides for the collection and analysis of costs by elements, functions, departments and jobs which enables the management to know the trend of costs and to control the efficiency of various operations, materials and machines by suitable comparisons.

(iii) By providing for collection and analysis of costs by elements, functions departments and jobs, job costing method provides a suitable basis for future planning and preparing quotations and estimates.

(iv) Job costing facilitates cost control through the comparison of actual costs with estimated costs.

(v) The recovery of overheads under job costing is generally made on the basis of pre-determined rates. This use of pre-determined rates necessitates the adoption of budgetary control of overhead. Thus, the manufacturing concern enjoys the advantages of budgetary control.

(vi) Spoilage and defective work can be easily identified with a specific job or work-order and the responsibility for the same can be fixed on departments and individuals.

8.5. LIMITATIONS OF JOB COSTING

Job costing method suffers from the following limitations:

(i) It involves too much clerical work which increases the chances of errors.

(ii) This method is historical in nature and thus fails to provide prompt remedial action in case of inefficiency.

(iii) Due to the recovery of overhead at pre-determined rates, job costing involves the problem of over/under-recovery of overhead.

(iv) The scheme of budgetary control may not be complete since it may not be extended to material and labour costs.

8.6. BATCH COSTING

Batch costing is a varied form of job costing. While job costing is concerned with the ascertainment of the cost of executing jobs by a jobber according the specifications given by the customers, batch costing is concerned with the ascertainment of the cost of a group of identical products manufactured for own stock. Batch costing is generally applied in the manufacture of medicines, component parts of complex products (such as motor cars, scooters, computers, watches, televisions, etc.), biscuits, food products, readymade garments, etc. The products manufactured in a batch are to be used for a particular purpose (e.g. spare parts of complex or composite products are to be used in a particular model only) or to be consumed within a specified period (e.g. medicines, biscuits and food products are to be consumed within a given period otherwise they become harmful).

For the purpose of costing each batch or group of identical products is allotted a serial number (known as batch number) just like a job number. The presentation of the various items of cost is made in the form of a statement known as "Batch Cost Sheet".

The batch sheet includes the cost of direct material, cost of direct labour and direct expenses which can be directly identified with a particular batch. The share of overhead chargeable to the batch (calculated on the same equitable basis) is also included the statement. The total cost of a batch as shown by the a batch cost sheet divided by the total number of products in the batch will give us the cost per product in the batch.

9

Process Costing

9.1. MEANING

Process costing is a method of costing used to ascertain the cost of a product at each stage or process of production. There are certain commodities which have to under to several distinct process of manufacture before completion. In such case it is desirable to find out the cost of product at the end of each such stage or process. This purpose is served by process costing. Process costing is usually employed in chemical works, soap making, oil refining, textiles, paper mills, biscuit works, food products, canning dairy, etc.

9.2. FEATURES OF PROCESS COSTING

The following are the features of process costing:

1. Under this method, a separate account is maintained for each process and each process is treated as a separate department.
2. Goods are manufactured in a continuous flow. Therefore, products lose their individual identity.
3. Products are transferred from one process to another till the goods are manufactured completely.
4. Cost of materials, wages and overheads are collected for each process and debited to the process account.
5. If by-products exist, their value should be credited to the process account in which they arise, so that the cost of that particular process is reduced.

6. The cost of a particular process is calculated by dividing the total cost incurred during a period by the number of units produced.

9.3. TREATMENT OF WASTAGE

Introduction: Waste is loss of material during the process of manufacture. It may be defined as that portion of basic raw material lost in processing; having no recovery value, anything which has no value is considered to be waste. In other words, waste has no value. The examples of waste are gases, dust, smoke and unsolvable residues. In process industries it is inevitable that each process causes some wastage.

In order to control waste, the following measures are taken in manufacturing concerns:

1. Waste report is prepared at regular intervals.
2. The actual percentage of waste is compared with standard percentage.
3. Holding of meetings with foreman and personnel regularly.

Treatment of wastage: Wastage may be normal or abnormal. Wastage may occur at the beginning of process, during a process or at the end of a process. Treatment or wastage is based on the distinction between normal and abnormal waste.

(a) Normal waste: It is the amount of loss which is unavoidable in a manufacturing process. It arises due to breakage, evaporation, deterioration, etc. The cost of normal wastage is distributed over goods output. It is treated as a cost of production. Where the wastage has some realizable value, the process account is credit with that realizable value.

(b) Abnormal waste: It is that part of loss which is unusual to the process and may arise due to some unforeseen factors. Abnormal waste arises due to inefficiency, mischief, bad luck, etc. Any wastage of materials in excess of the normal rate of wastage is known as abnormal wastage. The cost of abnormal waste is transferred from the process account to abnormal loss account. It cannot be treated as a financial loss. It can be controlled and avoided proper planning and efficiency management.

9.4. BY-PRODUCTS

Where one or more minor products are obtained in the process of manufacturing the main product, they are generally known as by-products. By-products are comparatively of much lower value than the main product, they difference from joint products in respect of production aim and relative from value and importance. By-products are defined as 'products of any saleable or useable value incidentally produced in addition to the main product'. In many process industries by-products are produced at different stages of production. In the oil refineries, for instance, in processing of crude petroleum yields not only refined oil but also other minor products such as sulphur, bitumen, chemical fertilizers, etc. Refined oil is the main product while minor products are by-products. In sugar industry, sugar is the main product whereas molasses and bagasseee are by-products. Some by-products are yielded in a saleable condition and others require further processing before they can be sold.

Treatment of by-products: The treatment of by-products in cost account depends upon the special conditions of each industry, the value of the by-products and the conditions in which they are yielded. The following are the different methods of treatment of by-products:

1. By-products of small value: Where by-products are of small value, the amount realised from the sale of them should be utilized in reducing the cost of the main product and credited to the account of the process from which they have been derived. For this purpose any expenses incurred in connection with the sale of by-products may be deducted from the sale proceeds while crediting the process account.

2. By-products of considerable value: In such cases the total expenditure unto the point of separation of the by-product from the main product must be apportioned between the main product and by-products. The main product is credited with the value placed upon the by produce and the by-product account is debited.

3. By-products which require further processing: In certain cases by-products are not yielded in a saleable condition and the manufacture has to incur further expenditure on them, before they can be sold. In such cases, the total expenditure up to the point of separating of the by-product from the main product must be apportioned between the main product and by-products. The by-products account is debited and the main product account is credit with the value of by-products. The by-products account will be further debited with the expenditure incurred in its processing.

9.5. JOINT PRODUCTS

In certain industries two or more products of equal economic importance are simultaneously produced. Such products are regarded as joint products thus, joint products represent two or more products. Severed in the costs of same processing each product being in such proportion that no single product can be designated as a major product, joint products imply the following:

1. They are produced from the same basic materials.
2. They are comparatively of equal importance.
3. They are produced simultaneously by a common process.
4. They may require further processing after the point of separation.

Different grades of coal extracted in a colliery, the meat and hides produced in a tannery, fuel oil, lubricants, coal tar, kerosene produced from petroleum are good examples of joint products the difference between a joint product and by-product is the relative significance of the product in comparison with the main product.

According of Joint Products

The basic problem in respect of joint products is that of apportioning the joint costs amongst the joint products on an equitable base. The following are some of the methods used in apportion joint costs.

1. Physical unit method: Under this method, the joint cost is apportioned on the basis of physical units of the respective joint products. The physical unit may be percentage of raw materials, unit or weight of products, volume of output, etc. This method however is not suitable where one product is gas and another a liquid and cannot be expressed in the same physical unit.

2. Market value method: Under this method, market value of the joint products at the separation point is ascertained and the joint cost is apportioned in the ratio of sales value or selling process. This method is simple and therefore is commonly used for the apportionment of expenses. However, it is not satisfactory, as it does not take into consideration the manufacturing and marketing costs incurred beyond the point of separation.

3. Survey method: Under this method, all the important factors such as volume, selling price, technical side, marketing process, etc. affecting costs are ascertained by means of extensive survey point values or percentage are given to individual products according to their relative importance and costs are apportioned on the basis of total costs. These ratios should be revised from time to time depending upon the factors affecting production and sales. This method is useful where joint products require further processing after separation.

9.6. DISTINGUISH BETWEEN PROCESS COSTING AND JOB COSTING

A comparative study of process and job costing will help in understanding the process costing system in a better way.

Process costing	Job costing
1. Costs are calculated process wise and per unit cost is the average cost ascertained by dividing the total cost of the process by the number of units produced.	1. Costs are separately calculated for each job, which is a cost unit.

Process costing	Job costing
2. Production of standardized and identical products is undertaken.	2. Production of non-standardized and evidential items is undertaken in accordance with the instructions and specifications of the customers.
3. Costs are calculated at the end of a particular period.	3. Costs are ascertained on the completion of a job.
4. As there are series of processes employed, the cost of one process is transferred to the other process.	4. As the job as a whole is considered as a single unit, there is no transfer of one part of job to another.
5. The nature of production is continuous, there is usually work-in-progress in the beginning as well as at the end.	5. The work-in-progress may or may not occur in the beginning and at the end of the accounting period.
6. On account of continuous and uninterrupted production, cost control is comparatively easier.	6. Cost control becomes difficult due to intermittent nature of production.
7. Production is taken to stores.	7. Production is undertaken against orders from the customers.

10

Reconciliation of Cost and Financial Accounts

10.1. MEANING OF RECONCILIATION

Reconciliation may be expressed as the process of tallying the working results or profits as shown by cost accounts with that of financial accounts. According to Eric L. Kohler, "Reconciliation is the determination of the items necessary to bring the balances of two or more related accounts or statements into agreement. Efforts are also made to judge the arithmetical accuracy of the profits revealed by two different sets of books." Thus, reconciliation of cost accounts and financial accounts involve the process of identifying and accounting for the items which have led to the difference in working results as shown by cost accounts and financial accounts. The reconciliation is made in an analytical form presented in the shape of a statement (known as Reconciliation Statement) or a memorandum account (known as Memorandum Reconciliation Account).

10.2. NEED FOR RECONCILIATION

The necessity for reconciliation of cost accounts and financial accounts arises due to the following reasons:

(i) Reconciliation assists in ascertaining the accuracy and reliability of the various sets of books of account maintained in a business concern.

(ii) It facilitates internal control since it discloses the reasons for the variation in profit or loss in an analytical manner.

(iii) It assists in effecting co-operation and co-ordination between costing office and accounting office.

(iv) It helps in formulating proper policies regarding overhead absorption, depreciation and stock valuation.

10.3. REASONS FOR RECONCILIATION STATEMENT

The discrepancy between the costing and financial results may be due to one or more of the following reasons:

1. Items shown only in financial accounts: There are a number of items which are included in financial accounts but find no place in cost accounts. These may be items of expenditure or items of income or appropriation of profits. These items may be classified as under:

(a) Purely financial charges

(i) Discount on debentures

(ii) Losses on the sale of fixed assets

(iii) Losses on investments

(iv) Interest on bank loans, mortgages and debentures

(v) Expenses of the company's share transfer office

(b) Purely financial incomes

(i) Profits on the sale of fixed assets

(ii) Transfer fees received

(iii) Dividend received

(iv) Interest received on bank deposits, loans, etc.

(v) Rent received

(vi) Commission received

(c) Appropriation of profits

(i) Income-tax and super taxes

(ii) Dividends paid

(iii) Transfers to reserves and sinking funds

(iv) Donations and charities

(v) Amounts written-off goodwill and preliminary expenses

2. Items shown only in cost account: There are certain items, which are included in cost accounts but not in financial accounts. These items are very few. These are usually notional charges. These items are:

(i) Interest on capital employed in production, though not paid.

(ii) Nominal rent charges of premises owned by the concern.

3. Over or under absorbed option of overhead in cost accounts: Overhead absorbed in cost accounts may be more or less than the actual amount spent. If overhead expenses in cost accounts are more than the actual. It is called over absorption. If overhead expenses in cost accounts are less than the actual, it is called under absorption of overheads and leads to difference in two accounts. In such a case costing profit will be higher and requires reconciliation.

4. Different bases of stock valuation of materials: In the financial accounts stocks are valued at cost or market price whichever is lower. But in cost accounts stocks of material are valued at cost. In financial accounts stocks of finished goods are usually valued at prime cost. In cost accounts, however, they are valued at prime cost plus appropriate proportion of production and administrative overheads. The difference in the basis of valuation of stocks of materials and finished goods may cause variations hence reconciliation is necessary.

5. Abnormal wastages: Abnormal wastage of material and time is included in financial account but excluded from cost accounts. Reconciliation of profit or loss of cost accounts with that of financial accounts is done by means of memorandum reconciliation or simply by reconciliation statement.

10.4. PREPARATION OF RECONCILIATION STATEMENT

Explain the procedure to be followed to prepare a reconciliation statement when there is a difference between the profits disclosed by cost accounts and financial accounts.

When there is a difference between the profits disclosed by cost accounts and financial accounts, the following steps shall be taken to prepare a reconciliation statement.

a. If profits per cost accounts (or loss as per financial accounts) is taken as the base.

Profit as per cost books.

Add

1. Over-charge or over-allocation or over-recovery of indirect expenses is cost books.
2. Receipts shown in financial books but excluded from cost books.
3. Over-valuation of opening stock in cost books.
4. Abnormal efficiency shown by financial accounts.
5. Items of expenditure such as interest on capital, rent on owned premises, etc. included in cost accounts but not in financial accounts.

Less

1. Under-charge or under-allocation of indirect expenses in cost books.
2. Items of expenditure included in financial accounts but not cost accounts.
3. Under-valuation of opening stock in cost books.
4. Cover-valuation of closing stock in cost books.
5. Abnormal wastage of time and material shown by financial books.
6. In terms of income included in cost accounts but not in financial accounts.

b. If profits as per financial accounts (or loss as per cost accounts) is taken as the base:

1. Items added above shall be deducted.
2. Items deducted above shall be added.

In simple the procedure adopted in 'a' case shall be reversed in 'b' case.

10.5. SPECIMEN OF RECONCILIATION STATEMENT

Profit as per Cost Accounts Rs.

Add:

(i) Over-recovery of overheads in Cost Accounts.

(ii) Items of Income/Receipts credited in Financial Accounts only.

(iii) Over-valuation of opening stock of Raw Materials, Work-in-Progress or Finished Goods in Cost Accounts.

(iv) Under-valuation of closing stock of Raw Materials, Work-in-Progress or Finished Goods in Cost Accounts.

Less:

(i) Under-recovery of overheads in Cost Accounts.

(ii) Items of Expenses/Losses debited in Financial Accounts only.

(iii) Under-valuation of Opening Stock of Raw Materials, Work-in-Progress or Finished Goods in Cost Accounts.

(iv) Over-valuation of closing stock of Raw Materials, Work-in-Progress or Finished Goods in Cost Accounts.

Profit as per Financial Accounts

10.6. MEMORANDUM RECONCILIATION ACCOUNT

Reconciliation of cost accounts and financial accounts may also be presented in the form of an account prepared on memorandum basis. Such an account is known as "Memorandum Reconciliation Account". The amount of profit as per cost accounts is shown on the credit side of this account. The various items to be added to the profit as per cost accounts, are credited to the Memorandum Reconciliation Account and the items to be deducted from profit as per cost accounts, are debited to it. The difference between the two sides of the account will reveal the amount of profit or loss as per financial accounts. The specimen of a Memorandum Reconciliation Account may be given as follows:

Memorandum Reconciliation Account

Particulars	Amt	Particulars	Amt
To Under-Recovery of Overhead in Cost Accounts.	?	By Profit as per Cost Accounts.	?
To Items of Expenses and Losses not included in Cost Accounts.	?	By Over Recovery of Overheads in Cost Accounts.	?
To Under-Valuation of Opening Stock in Cost Accounts.	?	By Item of Incomes and Receipts not included in Cost Accounts.	?
To Over-Valuation of Closing Stock in Cost Accounts.	?	By Over-Valuation of Opening Stock in Cost Accounts.	?
To Profit as per Financial Accounts.	?	By Valuation of Closing Stock in Cost Accounts.	?

11

Marginal Costing

11.1. DEFINITION OF MARGINAL COSTING

Marginal costing has been defined as the ascertainment, by differentiating between fixed costs and variable costs, of marginal costs and of the effect on profit of changes in the volume or type of output. Thus, under marginal costing, costs are classified under fixed and variable. In this method of costing, costs are classified under fixed and variable. In this method of costing only variable costs are charged to operations, processes or products while fixed costs are written off against profits in the period in which they arise.

Direct costing has been defined as "the practice of charging all direct costs to operations, processes or products, leaving all indirect costs to be written off against profits in the period in which they arise".

It should be noted that marginal costing and direct costing are treated as synonyms. These two terms convey the same meaning and are closely related. In U.S.A. the term direct costing is generally used, while in U.K the term marginal costing is used.

11.2. FEATURES OF MARGINAL COSTING

The following are the features of marginal costing:

1. In marginal costing, costs are classified under fixed and variable, variable costs only are charged to products. Fixed costs are written off to Profit and Loss Account during the period in which they are incurred.

2. Fixed overheads are mostly concerned with the period and are called period costs and hence they are transferred to Profit and Loss Account without carrying them to the next period through closing stocks. Variable costs very with the production and therefore, they are called "product costs" and charged to production.
3. Marginal costing is a technique of costing and is extensively used in all industries for profit planning, costs and decision-making.
4. Stocks of work-in-progress and finished goods are valued at marginal costs.
5. Marginal costing will help the management in fixing selling prices under different circumstances, such as trade depression, seasonal fluctuations in demand, etc.
6. In marginal costing actual fixed overhead is wholly charged to Profit and Loss Account. But in absorption costing system, fixed overheads can ever be absorbed exactly because of the difficulty in forecasting. Hence, there will be some difference in net profits.
7. Marginal costing helps the businessmen to reduce the price of a commodity in order to improve sales.

11.3. MEANING OF MARGINAL COSTING

Marginal costing is not a distinct method of ascertainment of costs such as the job or process costing. It is essentially a technique of cost analysis and cost presentation. It does not include fixed expenses. It includes only the prime cost and variable expenses. Since variable expenses only are included in this method of costing, it is also called direct costing, or variable costing. Marginal costing is defined as "the ascertainment of marginal cost and of the effect on profits of changes in the volume or type of output by differentiating between fixed costs and variable costs".

11.4. ADVANTAGES OF MARGINAL COSTING

The following are the advantages of marginal costing:

1. Marginal costing is a valuable aided to budgeting and standard costing.
2. It is simple to operate because it avoids the complexities of apportionment of fixed costs.
3. It helps the management for cost control and decision-making.
4. It helps the management in profit planning by break even charts and profit graphs.
5. It helps the management in flexing selling prices under different circumstances such as trade depression, seasonal fluctuations in demand, etc.
6. It avoids the complication of over-absorption and under-absorption of overheads.
7. It prevents the carry forward in stock valuation of some proportion of current years fixed overhead.
8. It helps the management to reduce the price in order to improve the sales.
9. In case of number of products are being manufactured, marginal costing facilitates the study of relative profitability of different products.

11.5. DISADVANTAGES OF MARGINAL COSTING

The following are the disadvantages of marginal costing:

1. The separation of costs into fixed and variable is difficult and sometimes gives misreading results.
2. It excludes fixed costs in taking important management decisions. Fixed expenses should be considered if the suitable comparison of two jobs is to be made.
3. Marginal costing is of no value if costs are to be taken for fixing selling prices.
4. It ignores the time factor as it excludes fixed expenses which are connected with time.

5. The application of variable overhead depends on estimates. So there is bound to be over or under recovery.
6. The technique of marginal costing is difficult to apply in industries such as ship-building or contracts where the value of work-in-progress is high in relation to turnover.
7. With the increased use of automatic machinery, the proportion of fixed costs increases. A system which ignores fixed costs is, therefore, less effective.
8. Marginal costing does not provide any standard for the evolution of performance. A system of budgetary control and standard costing gives more effective control than marginal costing.

In spite of the above disadvantages and limitations, marginal costing system is extensively used for cost control, profit planning and decision-making.

11.6. MANAGERIAL USES OF MARGINAL COSTING

Marginal costing is defined as the ascertainment by differentiating between fixed costs and variable cost, of marginal cost and of the effect on profits of changes in volume or type of output. This system is extensively used for cost control, profit planning and decision-making; it is essentially a technique of cost analysis and cost presentation. The information provided by the total cost methods may not be sufficient in solving the managerial problems. Sometimes the information provided by the total cost methods may be even misleading marginal cost system, on the other hand, provided sufficient information to the management, which aids the management in solving the managerial problems.

The following are some of the managerial problems which are simplified by the use of marginal costing:

1. Fixation of selling prices.
2. Make or buy decisions.
3. Key or limiting factor.

4. Effect of change in sales price.
5. Selection of a suitable product mix.
6. Maintaining a desired level of profits.
7. Alternative methods of production.

1. Fixation of selling prices: Although prices are controlled more by market conditions and other economic factors than by decision of management, the management, while fixing prices has to keep in view the level of profits expected. In normal circumstances, the fixed must cover total cost as otherwise profits cannot be earned. But under certain circumstances products may have to be sold at a price below, if such a step is necessary to meet the situation arising due to competition, trade depression, and additional order for utilizing spare capacity exploring new markets, etc. as a word of caution fixation of prices below total cost should be made only on a short-term basis. Marginal costing present's information regarding the rate of contributing at various levels of prices and capacity, so as to enable management to know the price limits within which it can operate.

2. Make or buy decisions: A concern can utilize its idle capacity by making component parts instead of buying them from market. In arriving at such a make or buy decision the price asked by the outside suppliers should be compared with the marginal cost of producing the component parts, if the marginal cost is lower than the price demanded by the outside suppliers, the component parts should be manufactured in the factory itself to utilize unused capacity. Further, the irregularity of the supply from outside source should also be kept in mind while taking such a make our buy decision.

3. Key factor: It is also called limiting factor. A key factor is that factor which puts a limit on production and profit of a business. Usually this limiting factor is sales a concern may not be able to sell as much as it can produces but production is limited due to the shortage of factors of production. In such a case, a decision has to be taken regarding the choice of the product which is to be increased, reduced or stopped. Ordinarily where there is no limiting factor, the choice of the product, will be on the basis of the highest P/V ratio. But when there are scarce or limited resources, selection of the product will be on the basis of contribution per unit of scarce factor of production.

4. Effect of change in sales price: Management is faced with the problem of cut in price of products from time to time on account of government regulations or competition. It is necessary, therefore, to know the effect of cut in price of the products.

5. Selection of a suitable product mix: When a concern manufactures more than one product, a problem often arises as to which product mix will give the maximum profits. The best product mix is one which yields the maximum contribution. Marginal costing helps the management in taking a decision to continue, increase, reduce or suspend production of a product or to huge the product mix.

6. Maintaining a desired level of profits: Management of a manufacturing concern may be interested in maintaining a desired level of profits. The volume of sales necessary to have a desired level of profits can be known by the marginal costing technique.

7. Alternative methods of production: Marginal costing is helpful in comparing the alternative methods of production. The method which gives the greatest contribution is to be adopted keeping the limiting factor in view.

11.7. CONTRIBUTION, MARGIN OF SAFETY, AND P/V RATIO

1. Contribution: The difference between sale value and marginal cost is called contribution or contribution margin. Contribution is regarded as share of that product in meeting fixed expenses and in profit. Contribution minus fixed expenses is not profit. Calculation of contribution helps in sales and pricing policies and measuring profitability of different proposals. As fixed expenses remain same, it is increase or decrease in contribution which causes increase or decrease in net profit. Contribution is a sure test to ascertain whether a product is worthwhile to choose among different products.

2. Margin of safety: The margin of safety is the difference between actual sales and the sales at the break-even volume is making no profit or loss. The margin of safety is small; any fall in sales may be a serious matter. A large margin of safety is unsatisfactory; steps must be taken to improve it. The following steps may be taken to improve an unsatisfactory margin of safety:

(a) Increase the level of production.

(b) Increase the selling price.

(c) Reduce the fixed or the variable costs or both.

(d) Substitute the existing product by more profitable products.

3. P/V Ratio: The profit volume ratio, usually called P/V ratio, is one of the most important ratios for studying the profitability of operations of a business. P/V ratio shows the relationship between the contribution, and the value of sales, it is an yardstick to measure the efficiency. It helps in determining break-even point, profit at any volume of sales, profitability of products, etc. Management always tries to improve the P/V ratio of each product. P/V ratio can be improved by increasing the selling price per unit or by increasing, the sales volume or by reducing the marginal cost. P/V ratio is also known as marginal income ratio, contribution to sales ratio or variable profit ratio.

11.8. BREAK-EVEN CHART

A break-even chart is a graphical representation of marginal costing. This chart shows the inter-relationship between profit volume and cost. These show the break-even point and also indicate the estimated profit or loss at varying levels of activity.

Assumptions Underlying Break-even Charts

1. All costs can be separated into fixed and variable costs.
2. Fixed costs will remain constant and will not change with change in output varies.
3. Variable costs will vary in the same proportion in which the volume of output varies.

4. Selling price will remain constant even though there may be competition or change in the volume of production.
5. There will no change in operating efficiency.
6. The number of units produced and sold will be the same so that there is no opening or closing stock.

Advantages of Break-even Charts

1. Break-even chart presents the information very clearly.
2. Break-even points and profitability of products can be known with the help of break-even chart.
3. The chart is very useful for forecasting costs and profits.
4. The chart is useful for studying the relationship of cost, volume and profit.
5. This chart is a tool for cost control because it shows the relative importance of the fixed costs and the variable costs.

Disadvantages of Break-even Charts

1. A break-even chart is based on a number of assumptions which may not hold good.
2. A limited amount of information can be shown in a break-even charts.
3. A break-even chart does not take into consideration capital employed. Therefore, managerial decisions, on the basis of break-even chart may not be reliable.
4. The effect of various product mixes on profit cannot be studied from a single break-even chart.

In spite of the above limitations, the break-even chart is a useful management device for analyzing the problems, if it is constructed and used by those who fully understand its limitations.

11.9. BREAK-EVEN POINT

Break-even point refers to the point where total cost is equal to total revenue. It is a point of no profit no loss. The points also known as the volume of operations where profits being. This is also the minimum point of production when total costs are recovered. In order to find out break-even point, costs can be stated in form of an equation.

Sales revenue at break-even point = Fixed costs + Variable cost

11.10. COST-VOLUME-PROFIT ANALYSIS

Cost-volume-profit analysis is very useful for management planning and control. It may be applied for profit planning, cost control and decision-making. Cost-volume-profit analysis is a technique used to establish and illustrate the inter-relationship between cost and profit at various levels of output. The higher the volume of output, the lower will be the unit of cost of production and vice versa. This is due to the presence of fixed overhead cost in the total cost, which does not raise or fall due to changes in the volume of output. Therefore, by separating fixed cost from the total cost, a direct relationship between variable cost and volume of output can be established, profit would increase as the volume of output is raised. If the sale price remains the same, profit would decrease, if the volume of output decreases. The higher the volume of output the lowers is the total unit cost and therefore, the profit is also higher. In cost-volume-profit analysis this fact is illustrated by means of marginal cost analysis and is represented by break-even charts. All items of costs are analyzed and classified into fixed cost and variable cost. The fixed cost remains fixed whatever may be the volume of output and variable cost is assumed to carry with the output. Therefore, the total cost for any projected output would be the aggregate of the fixed cost and the variable cost applicable to that level of output.

Objectives of Cost-Volume-Profit Analysis

This analysis may be applied for profit planning, cost control and decision-making. The following are the main objectives of such an analysis:

1. In order to forecast profit fairly and accurately, it is essential to know the relationship between profit and cost on the one hand and volume on the other.
2. Sales and costs vary with the volume of output. While establishing budgets for sales, and variable cots, it is necessary to budget the volume first. Cost-volume-profit analysis is useful in setting up flexible budgets which indicate costs at various levels of activity.
3. This analysis is of assistance in performance evaluation for purposes of control.
4. This analysis assist in formulating price policies. This enables the management in determining the selling prices of the product specially when demand for the product is elastic.
5. This analysis serves as a tool to enable management in taking appropriate decisions and formulating business policies.

Limitations and Assumptions of Cost-Volume-Profit Analysis

Cost-volume-profit analysis is made under certain limitations and certain assumed conditions. The main limitations and assumptions are as follows:

1. The analysis will be correct only if material prices, labour rates and selling prices remain constant.
2. This analysis is based on the assumption that all costs can be clearly separated into fixed and variable components. In practice, however, there are borderline case and types of costs which are partly fixed and partly variable in nature.
3. It assumes that fixed costs remain constant at all levels of activity. In practice this may not be so.
4. It assumes that variable costs are perfectly and completely variable at all the levels of activity. In practice this may not be so.

5. It is assumed that changes in the opening and closing stocks of finished goods are not significant. This also not holds good in practice.

In spite of the limitations the cost-volume-profit analysis is a useful management device, if it is constructed and used by those who fully understand its limitations. Scientifically prepared from reliable data, cost-volume-profit analysis will be a useful tool.

12

Uniform Costing

12.1. MEANING

Uniform costing is a system of costing under which several undertakings of the same industry adopt the same costing principles and practices. Uniform costing is not a separate technique or methods. It denotes a situation in which a number of undertakings of the same industry may use the same costing principles.

12.2. FACTORS REQUIRING CONSIDERATION UNDER UNIFORM COSTING

Where a uniform costing is introduced there must be some uniformity in the treatment of expenses and general accounting procedure. The important matters which require uniformity are as follows:

1. The basis for the apportionment and allocation of overheads.
2. The departments, sections to be used for analysis and comparison of costs.
3. What rates of depreciation shall be applied to plant and machines.
4. Whether interest on capital is to be included and if so how and on what basis.
5. What should be the treatment of wastages, scraps, by products, overtime, etc.
6. What should be the method of remunerating workers.

7. What rent charge is to be made for building if freehold or leasehold.
8. The demarcation between direct and indirect wages.
9. Items which should be excluded in cost accounts.
10. How expenses in connection with the buying, storing handling and issue of materials should be treated.

12.3. ADVANTAGES OF UNIFORM COSTING

1. Uniform costing provides a standardized method of collecting cost data.
2. It ensures that product prices are based on authentic data.
3. The operating efficiency of individual units and industry as a whole is improved as a result of continuous comparison of one with the other.
4. It simplifies the work of wage board set up for fixing the minimum wages or fair wages.
5. It provides reliable data for making inter-unit comparisons of cost performances.
6. It serves as a prerequisite to cost audit.

12.4. DISADVANTAGES OF UNIFORM COSTING

1. It is difficult to lay down standard principles and procedures as the size and types of businesses differ.
2. Many concerns do not disclose the figures to the trade association on the belief that confidential information will be disclosed to others.
3. Setting up of a uniform costing requires a high initial cost.
4. As the manufacturing methods differ from concern to concern, the standard principles and procedures fail to produce the desired results.

13

Budgetary Control

13.1. MEANING OF BUDGET

A budget is a plan of action expressed in figures. It is a planned estimate of future business conditions such as the income, probable cost and profit. It may be stated in financial terms or non-financial terms. It is defined as "a financial and/or quantitative statement prepared and approved prior to a defined period of time, of the policy to be pursued during that period of time, for the purpose of attaining a given objective". It may include income, expenditure and the employment of capital.

13.2. ESSENTIAL OF A BUDGET

A budget is an instrument of control. The following are the essentials of a budget:

1. It is prepared prior to a defined period of time.
2. It is prepared for the definite future period.
3. It may be stated in financial terms or non-financial terms.
4. It fixes a target in terms of rupees or quantities against which the actual performance is measured.
5. Before the preparation of the budget the policy to be followed to attain the given objectives must be laid down.

13.3. BUDGETARY CONTROL

Budgetary control is a system which uses budgets as a means of planning and controlling. The Institute of Cost and Works Accounts, London, defines budgetary control as "The establishment of budgets relating the responsibilities of executives to the requirements of a policy, and the continuous comparison of actual with budgeted results, either to secure by individual action the objectives of that policy or to provide a basis of its revision." According the J.A. Scott, "it is the system of management control and accounting in which all operations are forecasted and so far possible planned ahead, and the actual results compared with the forecasted and planned ones". In short, budgetary control implies department-wise planning, co-ordination of the various plans and the comparison of actual performance with the plan in order that any variations can be investigated and as far as possible remedied. Budgetary control provides management a strict control over the affairs of the business and improves efficiency and profitability.

Budgetary control involves the following:

1. Preparation of budgets for each function of the organization.
2. Recording of actual performance.
3. Continuous comparison of the actual performance with that of the budget.
4. Prompt investigation into differences.
5. Prompt remedial action when required.
6. Revision of budgets in the light of changed circumstances.

13.4. OBJECTIVES OF BUDGETARY CONTROL

The objectives of a budgetary control are as follows:

1. To plan and forecast the expenses and various activities of a concern.
2. To provide for co-ordination and control of activities and expenses.

3. To help department executives in systematically planning their activities and formulating policies to guide them in their work.
4. To determine the financial requirements in regard to the varied activities of the business from period to period.
5. To facilitate control over the different sections of the concern by means of section of expenditure under the various heads in advance.
6. To find out at periodical intervals, by comparison of the budget figures with those actually expended under each head, how far the actual results compare with pre-determined estimates.

13.5. ADVANTAGES OF BUDGETARY CONTROL

Budgetary control as now become an essential tool of the management for controlling costs and maximizing profit. It acts as friend, philosopher and guide to the management. It offers the following advantages:

1. Budgetary control secures efficiency and economy in the working of the business enterprise.
2. It establishes divisional and departmental responsibilities, it thus prevents "buck passing" when the budgeted results are not achieved.
3. It co-ordinates the activities of the various departments and functions by setting their limits and goals.
4. It ensures effective utilization of men, materials, machines and money.
5. It provides a yardstick against which actual performance of departments and employees can be compared.
6. It creates conditions for setting up a system of standard costing.
7. It assists a basis for internal audit by regular examination of departmental results.
8. It avoids over capitalization and under capitalization.
9. It acts as a safety signal for the management.

10. Managements which have developed a well order budget plan and which operate accordingly, received greater favour from credit agencies.
11. Budgetary control is helpful in reviewing current trends in the business and in determining future policy of the business.
12. It helps in promoting a feeling of cost consciousness and in restrictions expenditure to the minimum.

13.6. ESSENTIAL FEATURES OF AN EFFICIENT SYSTEM OF BUDGETARY CONTROL

Budgeting is one of the important control factors of management and therefore, successful implementation of budgetary control requirements certain essential features that they have to be streamlined before. They are:

1. The entire budgetary control programe must receive the active and whole-hearted support of top management.
2. The principles of formal organization and delegation of authority and responsibility must be applied at all levels of operation.
3. Responsibility and authority for budget preparation operation and supervision must be definitely determined and formally laid down. Delegation of budgetary responsibility must be consistent with delegation of operational responsibility.
4. The relationship between budgeting and accounting must be clearly defined.
5. There must be continuous budget education throughout the firm.
6. The uses and limitations of budgeting must be thoroughly appreciated and understood.
7. A thorough system of functions should be established to help management to forecast sales, process, costs and other trends which may furnish necessary information for preparing the budgets.

8. Cost records giving departmental expenses of present and past periods, and those comparing current performance as per the established budgets must be maintained.
9. Inspect and study the advantages and disadvantages of budgeting as they apply to the business of the firm.
10. Select the type of budget best suited to the business (fixed, variable or combined).
11. Decide the period for which the budget is adopted.
12. Draw up a classification of departmental budgets to, cover all important phases of the business.
13. Determine the steps for preparing and implementing the entire organization budget (Master Budget).

13.7. TYPES OF BUDGETS

Industrial concerns prepare different types of budgets for different purposes. Budgets may be prepared for short period of time or long period of time. Sales budget, production budget, materials budget, cash budget are some of the important types of budgets prepared.

13.8. VARIOUS FUNCTIONAL BUDGETS

The overall operational budget is customarily divides into number of functional budgets for the control of activities like sales, purchasing, production, materials, labour, manufacturing expenses, plant and equipment and finance.

1. Sales Budget

Budgeting starts with sales. The sales budget comes first because of its importance to both production and finance. To assist production and finance, the total sales budget should be expressed both in units of goods and volume of sales in rupees. The former acts as a guide to production and the later is the basis for the distribution of expenses and receipts. Since sales always represent the bulk of concerns income, they are obviously the determining factor in top managements budget decisions.

The cost of sales or sales expense is the other half of sale budget. Cost of selling is based to a large extent of previous sales volume. The average cost of unit of sales is the fundamental guide. Deviations from this norm would indicate whether the sales effort in particular area should be intensive or extensive.

Preparation of the sales budget starts with the men in field. If the company has a national distribution, salesmen's estimation are first received by the district sales manager's usual alterations should be made only after conferences with the salesmen concerned. After review by the district sales manager, a more objective criticism is made by the general sales manager and finally the estimates are reviewed by the district budget committee and chief executive. Some of the criteria which enter into revision of the field estimates are:

(a) Condition of the market
(b) Shifting populations
(c) Nature of population
(d) Purchasing power of various sections of the country
(e) Changes in consumers demand, bank deposits and scale of earnings
(f) The standard of living of population, etc.

2. Production Budget

The importance of production budget ranks second to sales. When the sales budget is divided into time periods, the scheduling of production of materially aided. The accuracy job sales forecasting helps placing large orders for materials and other inputs at advantageous price. When plant operations are maintained fully many savings would over. They are:

(a) Overtime work at previous wages rates may be avoided.
(b) Employment of study work force reduces training costs and maintain productivity at a higher level.
(c) Regular use of machinery reduces maintenance costs and improved productivity.

The production budget will be prepared on the basis of:

1. The sales forecast for the future one or two years.

2. The actual or estimated inventory on hand at the end of the period.
3. The standard inventory turnover.
4. The availability of working capital.

The production budget is drawn in order to achieve the anticipated sales and to maintain stock. The yearly budget is sales forecast plus or minus the increase or reduction of inventory required to bring the actual inventory to the level of the budgeted invented. When the overall budget for the output of the whole factory has been completed, this will be split up between various departments setting out forgets for each of them. Adequate arrangements to be made in advance for the supply of raw materials, labour and other stores that may be required for production process. Production budgets should indicate not only the quantity of production, but they should also show the time by which products are to be completed to meet the sales targets.

3. Materials Budget

Materials are divided into direct or indirect. Direct materials will enter into and becomes part of the production. Indirect material or auxiliary material cannot be traced as part of the product. It usually comprises materials required for operating and maintaining the plant and the equipment, oils, cotton waste, taps, and dyes, water belt, etc. These indirect materials are often included in a manufacturing expenses budget. The material budget depends largely on the materials called for in the production budget. Materials budget is useful not only to production but it is also useful to purchasing and financing sections. With the details of the materials budget, buying department can make its purchases efficiently and have its control over price, quality and delivery dates. Since purchases constitute large part of total costs, the material budget is important to the financing section for making available the cash to meet purchases in time.

A material budget will be prepared with the following details:

1. Cost of the raw material required.

2. The quantities of materials which must be in stock during each relevant period relating to production budget.
3. The dates by which materials required must be available.
4. The anticipated cost of the purchases to be made.
5. The period of credit obtainable from suppliers, etc.

4. Labour Budget

Labour is also classified as direct and indirect or productive and non-productive. Direct labours are labours that are engaged directly in the production process. Usually, indirect labour is not included in the production expenses budget. Labour requirements are expressed both in rupees and numbers, since labour estimates are used by the personal department for recruitment. The foreman for estimation estimates the amount of direct labour for various classifications; following details are taken into consideration:

(a) Labour turnover.

(b) The sales budget that suppliers the information of the number of workers needed in the various job classifications.

(c) The anticipated cost of such labour.

5. Production Expense Budget

Production or manufacturing expense is also known as factory overhead or our constituting number of items, which do not very proportionately with the volume of production. Examples of factory overhead are indirect labour, indirect materials, salaries to superintendent and foreman, material handling expenses, and clerical salaries, etc. It is important to know the relationship between the cost of those items and the volume overproduction. Cost accounting personnel and buying departments are very much interested in knowing the ratio of burden over the production or sales volume are some times important in connection with incentive payment. In many concerns the foremen's bonus payment depends not simply on the basis of his departments productivity but also on the amount by which he is able to reduce overhead or burden targets set for him in the budget.

This budget clearly shows the fixed and variable overheads. The fixed overheads refer to expenses which tend to remain constant or unaffected, while the variable overheads will increase or decrease according to output. So an estimate of variable overheads will have to be made for allocation to each production period keeping in view the estimated production for that period. Examples of fixed overheads are: rents, taxes, insurance, depreciation, salaries to officials, etc. Examples of variable overheads are maintained and repair charges small tools, consumable stores, idle time payment, overtime pay, lighting and heating administrative or office expenses, selling expenses and distribution expenses, etc.

6. Captial Expenditure Budget

Expenditure for expansion of plant, machinery and equipment are capital items for which budgetary planning is as important as for current items this budget usually requires long period than other budgets. Through this budget the resources of the enterprise are spent. Capital expenditure for the acquisition of fixed assets in the period ahead are planned and provided for through the prepare of this budget. When this budget is not used for execution of expansion programmed, unnecessary high costs would result in especially when sales are greatly increased. This budget would ensure the availability of capital at the rich time and it indicates the future capital expenditure over a long-run period.

7. Finance or Cash Budget

The financial budget includes a summary of all estimated receipts and expediture. It furnishes the overall control for top management guidance in the operations of the company. It shows the financial condition of the concern at the beginning or end of the budget period. This budget is the summary of the results of all other budgets showing the funds required in each production period to meet the anticipated expenditure in materials, wages, etc. It involves budget period. It serves as a guide in borrowing, in payment of dividends, in determining the transfer of profits to various reserves and funds, etc. It ensures steady supply of required working capital and current obligations of business. Some unusual heavy payments for the purchase of fixed assets, disbursement of interest, etc. can also be possible. Funds can be made available for purchasing of mate idle and goods.

13.9. FLEXIBLE BUDGET

This is also called variable budget or sliding scale budget. It may be defined as "a budget which is designed to change in accordance with the level of activity". It is prepared after making an intelligent classification of all expenses between fixed, semi-variable and variable. It is more elastic useful and practical. It takes into account the changes in the actual circumstances and it is useful for the purpose of control.

Desirability: The usefulness of flexible budget is highly appreciated in modern times. Flexible budget is specially desirable in the following cases:

1. Where sales cannot be predicted because of the nature of the business.
2. Where the business is subject to the vagaries of the weather.
3. Where progress depends upon an adequate supply of labour.
4. In the case of a new business, where it is impossible to forecast public demand.

Preparation: Flexible budgets are based on a clear distinction between fixed and variable costs. Before a flexible budget is prepared, each expense must be carefully analyzed and grouped into fixed, semi-variable and variable. Fixed expenses will tend to be unaffected by variations in the volume of output or sales semi-variable expenses will vary with variations in output or sales. Variable expenses will vary directly with variations in output of sales.

There are two alternative methods of preparing a flexible budget. They are multi-activity method, and formula method.

1. Multi-activity method: This method involves preparing budget figures for different levels of activity within a range; it takes into consideration the variable, some variable and fixed costs while computing the budget figures for different levels of activity. In the case of direct variable costs, the volume of production indicates the level of activity. However, in the care of overheads, the variability is known to be more in relation of time.

2. Formula method: This method is also known as budget cost allowance method. Under this method, budget first prepared for the expected normal level of activity, and provision is made for an allowance for variable costs per unit of activity for the number of units by which the actual level differs from the budget level.

13.10. RELATIONSHIP BETWEEN BUDGETARY CONTROL AND STANDARD COSTING

Budgetary control and standard costing are both invaluable aids to the management in controlling costs. Budgetary control is a system which uses budgets as a means of planning and controlling. It is defined as "the establishment of budgets relating the responsibilities of executives to be the requirements of a policy and the continuous comparison of actual with budgeted results, either to secure by individual action the objectives of that policy or to provide a basis for its revision". To say simply, budgetary control means comparison of actual costs with budgeted costs.

Standard Costing

Standard costing is a system of costs accounting which makes use of pre-determined standard costs relating to each element of cost. It is defined as "the preparation and use of standard costs, their comparison with the actual costs and analysis of variance to their causes and points of incidences".

Budgetary control and standard costing are inter-relating but not inter-dependent. In both systems targets are pre-determined actual performance is compared with the targets. Both are variable aids to management in controlling costs. Both the techniques are of importance in their respective fields. Both are complementary to each other. Budgets are usually based on past costs adjusted for likely future changes. In fact standards are often indispensable in the establishment of budgets. Such budgets may be termed as standard budgets. Similarly while setting standard overhead rates for standard costing purposes, the budgets fixed for the overhead costs may be made use of. The budgetary control system can, however, be operated without standard costing. But the operation of the standard costing system necessarily pre-supposes the existence of budgetary control. Usually the two systems are used in conjunction with each other to have most fruitful results. There are certain basis principles which are common to both the systems. They are:

1. The establishment of pre-determined targets of performance.
2. The measurement of actual performance.
3. The comparison of actual performance with the pre-determined targets.
4. The analysis of variances between the actual and the standard performance.

Thus, there is relationship between budgetary control and standard costing. Both are complementary to each other and for maximum efficiency both should be used simultaneously. Both are important tools for controlling costs.

13.11. DISTINGUISH BETWEEN BUDGETARY CONTROL AND STANDARD COSTING

Budgetary control and standard costing are valuable aids to the management for controlling costs. Both have the common objective of cost control by establishing pre-determined targets. The actual performances are measured and compared with the pre-determined targets for control purposes. Both are complementary to each other. The basic principles of cost control are common to both standard costing and budgetary control system. The two systems, however, vary in scope and in the matter of detailed techniques. The following are the important differences between the two systems:

1. Standards are based on technical assessments, whereas budgets are based on past actual adjusted to future trends.
2. Budget is a projection of financial accounts, whereas standard cost is a projection of cost accounts.
3. Budget are compiled for different functions of the business (purchases, sales, production, etc.). The expenses are classified as shown in the financial accounts. Standard costs, on the other hand, are compiled by classifying, recording and allocating expenses.
4. Budgetary control is concerned with the operation of the business as a whole. Hence, it is more extensive, standard costing, on the other hand, is more intensive. It is concerned only with the control of expenses.
5. Budgetary control does not necessarily involve standardisation of products. Standard costing, on the other hand, requires standardisation of products.
6. In budgetary control, variances are not normally revealed through the accounts. But under standard costing system, variances are revealed through different accounts.
7. Standards are set mainly for production and production expenses. But budgets are compiled for all items of income and expenditure.
8. Budgetary control can be adopted in part also. But it is not possible to operate standard costing system in parts.

Both standard costing and budgetary control are complementary to each other, and for maximum efficiency both should be used simultaneously. Both may prove more effective if they are used in conjunction with each other. Both are important tools for controlling costs.

14

Standard Costing

14.1. DEFINITION OF STANDARD COSTING

Standard costing is a very important system of cost control. Under this system, standard costs are set up and actual costs are compared with them. The differences or variances are calculated, and analyzed and remedial actions are taken. Thus, standard costing has been defined as the preparation and the use of standard costs, their comparison with the actual costs and analysis of variances to their causes and points of incidence.

14.2. SUITABILITY

The system of standard costing can be useful in all types of industries. The maximum benefit from the system is, however, obtained in industries producing standardized products which are repetitive in nature. This implies that they are of maximum value in process industries. Even in job industries where jobs offer from each other, there is a considerable scope for the use of this system of costing. Examples of industries where standard costing technique can be usefully employed are: cement, fertilizers, paper, electric lamps, biscuits, coral products, sugar, tobacco products, etc.

14.3. ADVANTAGES OF STANDARD COSTING

The short-comings of historical costing have led to the emergence of standard costing technique. Standard costing is a very useful managerial tool for cost control and cost reduction. The following are the main advantages:

1. Standard costing enables the management to ascertain the efficiency in various operations through comparison of actual and standard costs. This helps the management in exercising cost control.
2. It enables the management to utilize men, material and machines effectively. Thus, it may be led to economies and increased productivity in all business activities.
3. It provides a stable product cost per unit for guidance in price fixation.
4. It serves as a valuable aid to the management in formulating price and production policies. It helps management in preparing price lists, planning production of new products and furnishing cost estimates to higher levels.
5. It makes possible the application of the principle of management of exception. The management can concentrate its attention to cases of below or above standard performance.
6. It is more economical in clerical labour than any other method for providing the management with the same kind of information.
7. It simplifies the cost control procedure and thereby reduces the cost of cost accounting.
8. It creates an atmosphere of cost consciousness among executives, foremen, and workers. This increases efficiency and productivity all round.
9. It provides complete integration of cost and financial accounts without the need to any kind of reconciliation between separate sets of accounts.
10. It makes possible an effective delegation of authority.

14.4. DISADVANTAGES OR LIMITATIONS OF STANDARD COSTING

The following are the disadvantages of standard costing:

1. The technique of standard costing may not be applicable in case of small concerns because establishment of

standards requires high degree of skill. Thus, fixation of standards may prove costly which a small organisation may not afford.

2. The division of variances into controllable and uncontrollable variances is a difficult task.
3. The technique of standard costing may not be very effective in the industries which deal with non-standardized products and the jobs which change according to customer's requirements.

14.5. DISTINGUISH BETWEEN STANDARD COSTS AND ESTIMATED COSTS

Standard cost is a pre-determined cost. It has been defined as 'a pre-determined cost which is computed in advance of production on the basis of a specification of all the factors affecting costs and used in standard costing'. In other words, standard cost is a pre-determined cost that should be attained under a set of operating conditions.

Standard costs and estimated costs are pre-determined costs, but their objectives are different. The main differences between these two types of costs are as follows:

1. Estimated cost is more or less a reasonable assessment of what a cost 'will be', whereas standard cost is a specification of what a cost 'should be'.
2. Estimated costs are based on expected actual and the average of the past performance. Standard costs, on the other hand, are planned costs. They are determined on scientific basis.
3. Estimated costs are used by concerns which follow historical costing system. But standard costs are used by concerns which follow standard costing system.
4. Estimated costs are used only as statistical information and are not entered in the books. But standard costs are entered in the regular system of accounts.
5. Estimated costs do not serve the purpose of cost control. They serve other purposes such as fixation of prices. But

standard costs lay emphasis on cost control. They serve as yardsticks against which actual performance can be measured.

14.6. VARIANCE

Variance means difference. In standard costing variance means difference between standard specified and actual result. In other words, the deviation of the actual cost or profit or sales from the standard cost or profit or sales is known as variance. Variance may be favorable or unfavorable. When actual cost is less than the standard cost, the difference is known as favorable or credit variance. When actual cost is more than standard cost, the difference is known as unfavorable or debit variance. In other words, any variance that increases the actual profits is favorable and any variance that decreases the actual profits is unfavorable.

There are number of reasons which give rise to variances. The analysis of variances will help to locate the reason, and person or department responsible for a particular variance. The analysis of variance will further reveal that some of the variances are controllable while others are uncontrollable. Cost control is exercised ascertaining and analyzing the variances and taking immediate corrective steps.

Kinds of Variances

The variances are generally divided into material variances, labour variances, overhead variances, and sales variances. Each of these are further sub-divided into a number of variances.

(a) **Material variances:** This is the difference between the standard cost of materials specified and the actual cost of materials used. This may arise on account of change in price of materials or change in quantity or both. The variance in material cost is generally divided into the following variances:

1. Material price variance: This represents the differences between the standard quantity specified and the actual quantity used.

2. Material quantity variance: This represents the difference between the standard quantity specified and the actual quantity used.

3. Material mix variance: This represents the difference between the standard mixture and the actual mixture of different materials.

4. Material yield variance: This represents the difference between the standard yield of finished product and the actual yield thereof.

(b) **Labour variance:** This is the difference between the standard wages specified for the activity achieved and the actual direct wages paid. This may arise on account of difference either in rates of wages of time. This is sub-divided into the following variances:

1. Labour rate of pay variance: This represents the differences between the standard labour hours and the actual labour hours expended.

2. Labour mix variance: This is also called Gang composition variance. This is like labour mix variance. This arises if during a particular period the grades of labour used in production are different from those specified.

3. Labour idle time variance: This arises when there is a difference between the time for which workers are paid and that which they actually expend upon production.

(c) **Overhead variance:** This is the difference between the standard costs of overheads allowed for the actual output achieved the actual overhead cost incurred. In other words, overhead cost variance is under or over absorption of overheads. Generally variance in overhead costs are divided into (a) variable overhead variance, and (b) fixed overhead variance.

Variable overhead variance is the difference between standard and actual variable overheads. Fixed overhead variance is the difference between standard and actual fixed overheads. Overhead variance is further sub-divided into the following variances:

1. Expenditure variance: This represents the difference between the standard expenses and the actual expenses incurred.

2. Volume variance: This represents the difference between budgeted production and actual production.

3. Efficiency variance: This represents the difference between standard production and actual production.

4. Capacity variance: This represents the difference between budgeted quantity and standard quantity.

5. Yield variance: This represents the variance in fixed overhead caused by material yield variance.

6. Calendar variance: This represents the difference between budgeted hours and possible hours of production.

(d) **Sales variance:** Sales variance may be sub-divided into the following variance:

1. Sales value variance: This represents the difference between the standard value and the actual value of sales affected during a period.

2. Sales price variance: This represents the difference between actual price and standard price specified.

3. Sales volume variance: This represents the difference between actual quantity of sales and standard quantity of sales.

4. Sales mix variance: This represents the difference in the proportion in which various articles are sold and the standard proportion in which various articles were to be sold.

15

Operating or Service Costing

15.1. OPERATING COSTING

Operating costing could well be considered as refinement of single costing. It is adopted by those businesses which operate a service rather than produce goods. Service is their final product and their main feature. This service may be sold by the enterprises to consumers. Typical examples of these are railways, bus companies, tramways, airways and shipping companies, hotels, motels, banking, finance and consultancy firms, electricity boards, gas, water and other public utility undertakings. This service may also be used within the enterprise as is the case with cafeteria, boiler house maintenance, etc. Operating costing, therefore, is a method which seeks to determine the cost of services being rendered. Here the costing division is an operation, not a job or a process.

In operating costing, the cost unit is also a single unit. But it is less tangible than a job or product. It is a composite or compound unit of cost and consists of two or more statistical factors, each of which has some relationship with the service performed. The examples are the following:

(i) cost per mile or cost per hour of running,

(ii) cost per tonne mile,

(iii) cost per package carried,

(iv) cost per trip where standard products are carried out,

(v) bed-day/patient-day,

(vi) kilowatt-hour.

It would be noticed that passengers and goods are considered here from the view point both of numbers and distance. The cost of carrying two passengers for two kilometers four times the cost of carrying one passenger for one kilometer.

15.2. TRANSPORT COSTING

Transport is one of the services performed by railways, roadways, steamers, goods carriers, etc. Such businesses adopt operating costing for the purpose of finding the total cost of each vehicle and then applying it to the unit cost. The cost information helps in charging for the service against departments and outside customers. It also helps in making comparison among the vehicles and then applying it to the unit cost. The cost information helps in charging for the service against departments and outside customers. It also helps in making comparison among the vehicles and alternative modes of transport. However, the service provided by the transport carriers depends upon:

(a) the scientific routing of vehicles so that deliveries for adjacent customers are combined and 'light loading' reduced to the minimum,

(b) the use of vehicles of appropriate type and capacity,

(c) the supervision of the time taken for journeys of known mileage, and

(d) the possibility of return loads so that empty return journeys are minimized.

15.3. STANDING CHARGES

Standing charges is a collective name for all the expenses which have to be incurred whether the vehicle operates or not. The vehicle may be idle, but even then its expenses have to be met. These are more or less fixed in nature in a transport company. The typical items of standing charges are:

(i) Road license fees

(ii) Insurance premium

(iii) Interest on capital

(iv) Garage rent or an allowance therefore

(v) Apportionment of supervision costs
(vi) Depreciation.

15.4. OPERATING AND RUNNING COSTS

These are just the opposite of standing charges. The expenses which are incurred on the actual running of the vehicles are so called. These vary from day to day and come to zero when the vehicles are off the road. These are variable in nature and the examples of these are the following:

(i) Petrol and fuel
(ii) Oil and grease
(iii) Wages of driver (not necessarily wholly).

15.5. MAINTENANCE CHARGES

These expenses are incurred on the repairs and maintenance of vehicles so as to keep them in proper gear. They are semi-variable in nature and the examples thereof are:

(i) Wear and tear of tyres
(ii) Repairs and overhauls
(iii) Painting
(iv) Hire of spare vehicles when the firm's own are under repair.

15.6. LOG SHEET

A log book is maintained in respect of each vehicle, generator, or pumping set. It records various details during a given period of time. For working out the cost of services, it is important to know the capital maintenance and running cost, trips made, fuel and oil supplied, worker's time spent and exceptional delays. These particulars enable the management to make suitable allocation of vehicles and thus avoid waste or idle running capacity and unnecessary or duplicate trips. It is usually divided into three parts. The second part furnishes the cost of maintaining the services, and the third part gives the essential information for the computation and control of the operating costs.

16

Cost Audit

16.1. MEANING

Audit may be described as a systematic examination of the books, vouchers and records of a business to enable the auditor to satisfy himself and to report whether the accounts thereof are properly drawn up so as to exhibit a true and fair view of the state of affairs of the business. Initially, the scope of audit was limited to the verification of the transactions of financial nature but in the recent times, it has been extended to other fields also. Cost audit is one of them. Cost audit is concerned with the verification of the correctness of the cost records or cost accounts maintained in a business concern.

On the basis of the analysis of the above definitions, it can be said that cost audit is the detailed checking as well as the verification of the correctness of costing techniques, systems and cost accounts. In any manufacturing concern or in a service organization, it is generally felt necessary to compute the correct cost of products or services so as to charge the customers correctly. For this purpose, cost accounts or costing records are maintained. But only the maintenance of cost accounts is not sufficient. In order to ascertain the true and accurate cost of products and services, it is necessary to ensure that these records are accurate and correct. As such there is a need to get the costing records properly audited and checked by a properly qualified and trained professional.

16.2. OBJECTIVES OF COST AUDIT

The main objectives of cost audit are:

(i) To verify that the cost accounting records (or costing books) are accurate.

(ii) To certify that costing principles have been fully adhered to in maintaining cost accounts.

(iii) To find out whether the pre-determined cost accounting procedures and processes have been strictly followed by the management.

(iv) To detect errors and frauds, which might have been committed intentionally or otherwise in preparing cost accounts.

(v) To check whether each item of expenditure involved into the relevant components of goods manufactures has been properly incurred.

(vi) To see how far the existing practices of cost records are helpful for the management to take decisions.

(vii) To disclose the deficiencies or inefficiencies in the use of material, labour and machines with a view to assist the management.

(viii) To assist the external auditor in conducting detailed checking by reducing the volume of audit work through the use of internal cost audit system.

(ix) To exercise moral check on the cost accounting staff and to attain efficiency in cost accounting systems and procedures.

16.3. SCOPE OF COST AUDIT

The scope of audit has two important aspects viz.:

(i) Propriety audit.

(ii) Efficiency audit.

(i) Propriety audit: This aspect of audit is concerned with actions and plans of management which affect the finance and expenditure of the business concern. Under this aspect, the cost auditor is required to ensure that an item of expenditure is sanctioned or approved by the proper authority. It is done with the help of documents and vouchers. In addition, the cost auditor has to ensure that an item of expenditure is sanctioned or approved by the proper authority. It is done with the help of documents and vouchers. In addition, the cost auditor has to ensure that the item of expenditure is proper and reasonable on the grounds of propriety. Thus, the cost auditor has to report:

(a) Whether or not the planned expenditure could give optimum results.

(b) Whether or not the size or channels of investment were designed to produce the best results.

(c) Whether the return from investment in certain channels could be bettered by some alternative plan of action.

(ii) Efficiency audit: This aspect of cost audit is concerned with the evaluation of performances. It covers the verification of the facts that the exenditure has been incurred according to the plan and the results obtained have also been according to the plan. It covers the examination of the plan prepared in the form of budgets (financial and functional) and the comparison of the actual performance with the budgeted performance and analyzing the reasons for variances. Thus, efficiency audit ensures that:

(a) Every rupee invested in capital or in other fields gives the optimum return; and

(b) Investment in different spheres of the business has been so balanced that it gives maximum results.

Therefore, the cost auditor plays the role both as consultant and financial adviser. He assists the chief executive of the business concern in judging the soundness of the financial plans and performances by co-ordination the results of actions of heads of various departments.

16.4. DISTINCTION BETWEEN COST AUDIT AND FINANCIAL AUDIT

It is difficult to make a distinction between cost audit and financial audit from the practical point of view though in principle the difference does exist. The main points of distinction between cost audit and financial audit may be summarized as follows:

1. Audit of the financial accounts is compulsory under the provisions of the Companies Act while cost audit is not compulsory except in the case of companies carrying on manufacturing or mining business which have been specifically required to maintain cost accounts under Section 209(1)(d) and get them audited under Section 233.
2. The main object of the financial audit is to see whether the accounts of the business have been properly maintained and whether the Profit and Loss Account and Balance Sheet exhibit a true and fair position of the state of affairs while in case of cost audit the auditor has to examine whether the expenditure involved has been wisely incurred or not and to find out the cost of manufacture of each unit of articles.
3. In case of financial audit, the auditor has to examine the financial accounts such as capital, debtors, creditors, assets, liabilities, expenses and income, etc. and he does not go into the details of cost records but the cost auditor has to go into the details of cost records to detect errors and manipulation in cost accounts.
4. In respect of closing stock the financial auditor has to see whether it has been correctly valued for the purpose of inclusion in Balance Sheet while the cost auditor has to see whether the stock is excessive or otherwise keeping in view the needs of the manufacturing concern.
5. In case of financial audit, the auditor examines the financial aspect of accounts while the cost auditor is concerned with the cost aspect of accounts.
6. The financial auditor has to certify the arithmetical accuracy of the transactions in proper books of accounts relating to cash receipts and payments, purchases and sales and assets and liabilities while the cost auditor has to certify the facts relating to the utilization of material, labour and other services.

16.5. FUNCTIONS OF COST AUDIT

The functions and areas of cost audit as given in the booklet named *Cost Audit, Its Significance* issued by the Institute of Cost and Work Accountants of India may be summarized as follows:

1. Inventory

The cost Auditor will examine, inter alias, the following:

(a) Is the size of inventory adequate or excessive compared with the production programmed?

(b) Is the provisioning drill most economical?

(c) Does it ensure optimum order size?

(d) Does it take into account the storage cost on the one hand, and carrying cost on the other?

(e) Does it take note of lead-time of the various items or group of items?

(f) Does the receipt and issue system cause any bottleneck in production?

(g) Does it involve too many forms and too much paper work?

(h) Is there any room for reduction of inventory cost consistent with production needs?

(i) Is there inventory as per the priced store ledger and as certified by the management physically correct?

(j) Is the same amount of attention and care given to moneys translated into material things like raw materials, stores and supplies of all kinds as is given to liquid cash?

(k) Does the issue of raw materials make the production in accordance with the standard or schedule or otherwise or covered by authorized schedule?

(l) Is the expenditure of consumable stores within the standard? If not, why not?

2. Operating and Closing Stock

The cost Auditor will see, inter alias, the following:

(a) that the opening stock is not unduly large compared with the volume of production during the year;

(b) that the opening stock against various jobs does really represent the actual physical stock in the production shop and is not merely an accounting figure;

(c) that the responsibility of the shop-foreman-in-charge of the stock held in the production shop is clear an properly documented; that he maintains proper record of actual consumption vis-à-vis the actual withdrawal from the stock;

(d) that the physical verification is correctly carried out;

(e) that the valuating is correct with reference to the actual cost of production and recognized policy for valuation;

(f) that the volume of closing stock is commensurate with the volume of production and that it does not reflect any failure or bottleneck in sales budget or production budget;

(g) that the volume of unmoved stores is not abnormal in comparison with the normal rate of yearly consumption. The cost Auditor will recommend disposal of such unmoved stores with consequent release of capital unnecessarily locked up to the advantage of the financial resources of the concern.

3. Stores Issues Procedure

The cost Auditor will see, inter alias:

(a) that withdrawal of materials from stores by production shop is scientific or covered by authorized schedule and permits receipts to be located;

(b) that there is no possibility of loss of pilferage of stock lying in the production sections;

(c) that surplus materials and scalps arising in production shops are returned to stores correctly and without delay for which necessary credit is given to unit cost of production. If transferred to other jobs, proper transfer voucher has been prepared and copies sent to the accounts, stores, etc.

4. Work-in-Progress

The cost Auditor will ensure, inter alias, the following:

(a) that the work-in-progress has been physically verified and that it agrees with the balance in the incomplete cost card;

(b) that the valuation of the work-in-progress is correct with reference to the stage of completion of each job or process and the value booked in the job cost cards or process cost sheet;

(c) that there is no over-valuation or under-valuation of opening or closing work-in-progress, thereby artificially pushing up or down net profits or net assets as the case may be;

(d) that the volume and value of work-in-progress is not disproportionate compared with the finished out-turn.

5. Labour

Proper utilization of labour and increase in productivity are now receiving greater attention. Several productivity teams have emphasized great importance of higher productivity. It is therefore, essential to assess performance efficiency of labour and compare it with the standard performance, so that labour utilization could be progressively improved. Labour force in Indian industries is generally very high compared to similar types of industries in other developed countries. Our aim should be to reach that level, though necessarily not immediately but over a period. A study of this nature would give an idea where inefficiency lies so that timely and adequate steps could be taken to ensure maximum utilisation of labour and to reduce labour cost.

6. Capacity Utilization

The cost Auditor will see, inter alias,

(a) that the idle capacity in any production shops or of transport facilities for distribution is not excessive;

(b) that production volume and overall machine time utilized are commensurate. In other words, the machine hours utilized have given the optimum out-turn.

7. Overheads

The cost Auditor will see and certify, inter alias,

(a) that allocation of indirect expenditure over production, sales, and distribution is logical and correct that compared with the volume of production in a production shop, the overhead charges are not excessive;

(b) that compared with the volume of production in a production shop, the overhead charges are not excessive;

(c) that the actual indirect expenditure does not exceed budgets or standard expenditure significantly and that any variations are satisfactorily explained and accounted for;

(d) that the relation of indirect expenditure in keeping with the load on individual production shop is appropriate;

(e) that allocation of overheads between finished and unfinished products is in accordance with correct costing principles.

8. Capital Expenditure

The cost Auditor will see and certify, inter alias,

(a) that the purchase of new plant and machinery is duly authorized;

(b) that the capital expenditure has been regularly collected;

(c) that the actual progress of capital expenditure is according to the budget;

(d) that the capital expenditure is profitable; and

(e) that the fixed assets and proper maintenance of plant records have been physically verified.

16.6. TYPES OF COST AUDIT

The following are the different types of cost audit:

1. Cost audit on behalf of management: Cost audit on behalf of management is a part of general internal control measure. Depending on the size of the organization and the importance of cost accounts a separate cost audit department is set up to ensure that the costing records are accurate and compiled correctly to facilitate cost ascertainment and cost control and to ascertain whether the cost procedures and routines pricing of stores, allocation of overhead expenses, etc. are being uniformly followed.

2. Cost audit on behalf of a customer: Sometimes the contracts and orders are placed on 'Cost-plus' basis. In such a case the price is based on cost plus an agreed margin of profit. The customer, in such a case, may get the cost accounts audited in order to establish the accuracy of cost.

3. Cost audit on behalf of labour tribunals: Sometimes a labour Tribunal may get the cost accounts of a manufacturing concern audited for deciding labour's claim for higher wages, bonus and share in profits, etc.

4. Cost audit on behalf of government: Government may get the cost accounts of a manufacturing concern audited for the following reasons:

(i) for fixing fair prices of some commodities so as to prevent over profiteering;

(ii) for providing protection to certain industries;

(iii) for fixing the price of cost plus contracts given to private contractors.

5. Cost audit under the Companies Act: Under the Companies (Amendment) Act, 1965, two new amendments have been added to the Companies Act, 1956 in this respect, clause to sub-section (1) of Sections 209 and 233B to Section 233 which provided for the audit of cost accounts in certain cases. According to Section 209(1)(d), every company shall keep at its registered office proper books of accounts with respect to—

> In the case of a company pertaining to any class of companies engaged in production, processing, manufacturing or mining activities, such particulars relating to utilization of materials or labour or as to other items of cost as may be prescribed, if such class of companies is required by the Central Government to include such particulars in the books of account.

It would be observed that the cost audit can be ordered in case of those companies which are required to maintain cost accounts under Section 209(1)(d) cited above and which are engaged in production, processing, manufacturing or mining activities. More and more companies are now asked under Section 23B to get their cost accounts audited.

Question Bank

COST CONCEPT AND PRINCIPLES

1. What do you understand by "Cost Accounting"? Discus the main advantages.
2. Explain the terms "costing", "cost accounting" and "cost accountancy".
3. What is meant by "Cost Accounting"? What are its advantages?
4. Define "Costing" and discuss briefly its objects and advantages.
5. "A good costing system is an invaluable aid to management". Enumerate the chief points in support to this statement.
6. "Cost Accounting has come to be an essential tool management." Give your comments on this statement.
7. "Cost Accounts are the key to economy in manufacture and are indispensable to the intelligent and economical management of a factory". Discuss.
8. Explain how costing helps to promote the efficiency of management of a factory?
9. Summaries the advantages which management may derive from a complete system of cost accounting.
10. What are the objections raised against costing?
11. Discuss the main objections that are advanced against costing system?
12. What are the main functions of a costing system?

13. What are the functions and characteristics of a good cost accounting system?
14. What are the essentials of a good system of costing?
15. What are the characteristics of an ideal cost accounts system?
16. What is cost accounting? In what respects does it differ from financial accounting?
17. Distinguish clearly between cost accounts and financial accounts.
18. Why are cost accounts necessary and in what respects do they differ from the ordinary financial accounts?
19. Distinguish between cost accounts and financial accounts. What information can be obtained from the former that cannot be obtained from usual financial accounts?
20. In what ways cost accounting system is superior of financial accounting system?
21. "The ordinary trading account is a locked store house of most valuable information to which cost is the key". Elucidate the above statement and explain the difference between financial and cost accounts.
22. How does cost accounting differ in technique and procedure from financial accounting?
23. Discuss the limitations and deficiencies of financial accounts.
24. What are the pre-conditions that are to be observed before installing a good costing system?
25. Describe briefly the preliminary steps you would take if you were asked to introduced a costing system is factory.
26. Describe the general conditions that should be observed for the efficient introduction of a costing system.
27. As a cost accountant what are the general conditions you will observe when installing costing system in an organization?
28. "Costing is a mere approximation of figure". Discuss.

29. Discuss the statement that "Costing is a mere approximation of expenses".
30. "Costing is merely a system of estimates". Critical examine the statement.
31. "A good system of costing serves as means of control over expenditure and helps to secure economy in manufacture". Explain the statement.
32. Discuss the relationship between cost accounting and management accounting. Enumerate the chief features of management accountancy.
33. "An estimate is an opinion, price is a policy and cost is a fact". Discuss?
34. Distinguish between (a) estimates, (b) costs, (c) price, and indicate how they are related to each other?
35. Describe briefly the different techniques of costing.

ELEMENTS OF COST

1. Explain the various constituent "Elements of cost making up the total cost of sales"?
2. Enumerate the heads under which expenditure is usually classified and grouped. Show such classification by means of a chart.
3. Discuss the various elements of cost. Give a few examples of each.
4. Define the following and give the alternative names by which each is known:
   (a) Prime cost
   (b) Works cost
   (c) Office cost
   (d) Total cost
5. Discuss the various ways in which costs may be classified.
6. "Cost may be classified according to their nature and a number of other characteristics". Discuss this statement while classifying costs.

7. What do you understand by 'Unit of cost'? What is the proper unit of cost for the following:
   1. Contractors
   2. Hotels
   3. Sugar mills
   4. Collieries
   5. Oil refinery
   6. Water works
   7. Textile mills
   8. Brick works
   9. Transport companies
   10. Electricity companies
   11. Breweries
   12. Flour mills
   13. Paper mills
   14. Press work
8. Explain
   (a) Cost Center
   (b) Cost Audit
   (c) Cost plus Costing
9. Write short notes on the following:
   1. Imputed cost
   2. Shut-down and sunk costs.
10. Describe the different methods of costing and state the particular industries to which they can be applied.
11. Explain the different methods of costing briefly and name the industries to which they are applicable.

    What methods of costing would you apply to the following industries and why?
    (a) Brick works
    (b) Motorcar manufacture
    (c) Motorcar service
    (d) Biscuit manufacture.
12. State with reasons the method of costing that is recommended for the use of the following:
    (a) Chemical Works
    (b) House Building
    (c) Bricks
    (d) Passenger Buses.
13. What method of costing would you apply to the following and why?
    (a) Printers and publishers
    (b) Boot and shoe manufactures

(c) Motorbus service
(d) Spinning and weaving mills
(e) Soap manufactures.

14. State what method of costing will you apply in each of the following cases:
    (a) Motorcar manufacturing
    (b) Electricity supplying
    (c) Coal mining
    (d) Brewery.
15. Mention with reasons the type of costing you will adopt in the following industries
    (a) Cement manufacturing
    (b) Railways
    (c) Shipbuilding
    (d) Bicycle manufacturing
    (e) Readymade garments.
16. What are the items of expenses and incomes which are excluded from cost accounts?

MATERIAL

1. What do you understand by the term 'Material control'? What are the advantages of material control?
2. What do you understand by "Material control"? What are the essential features of material?
3. What is "Material control"? Mention the requisites of an adequate system of material control. What advantages may be obtained from a good system of material control?
4. What do you understand by "Inventory control"? State its main purposes.
5. Discuss the functions of the purchasing department?
6. Describe fully the procedure in Purchasing receiving and accounting of materials.

7. What is a purchase requisition? Give a specimen form of purchase requisition and state the information contained therein.
8. What information should appear on a purchase requisition? Give a specimen form.
9. What is purchase order? To whom should the copies of purchase order be sent and why? Give a specimen form of the purchase order.
10. Define bill (or specification) of materials and outline a form with reference to an industry with which you are familiar. Mention the purposes served by the same in
    (a) Stores (b) Production and
    (c) Accounts department.
11. What is a goods received note? Give a specimen form and state what purpose does it serve?
12. Discuss the importance of good storekeeping in an organization. What are the duties of storekeeper?
13. What are the matters to be considered while establishing a good stores department?
14. Discuss relative advantages and disadvantages of
    (a) Central Stores (b) Sub-Stores.
15. Describe (a) Bin Card (b) Material Return Note.
16. Explain the procedure of continuous stock-taking and its advantages over annual stock-taking.
17. What is meant by 'perpetual inventory'? What are its advantages over periodical inventory?
18. Describe the perpetual inventory system and explain its advantages and disadvantages.
19. What do you understand by 'perpetual inventory system? What are the advantages and how is it applied?
20. Describe a system that would give you quickly the value of closing stock and work-in-progress at the end of financial period without least delay. Enumerate and explain in the

main methods used in cost accounts for the pricing of material issued to jobs.

21. "Stores Ledgers are essential to an efficient costing system". Comment on this statement and state the use and value of stores ledger.
22. What useful purposes are served by the stores ledger? Give a ruling for it and show at least half a dozen illustrative entries.
23. Explain what is meant by 'minimum level', 'maximum level', and 'ordinary level' with regard to maintenance of stock? What are the factors that given the fixing up of these levels?
24. Define the following and explain on what basis each should be determined:
    (a) Maximum Stock (b) Minimum Stock
    (c) Ordinary Level (d) Ordering Quantity.
25. Describe the factors that are to be considered while determining the maximum level, minimum level and ordering level. State the important of levels setting from the point of stocks control.
26. Distinguish between scrap; spoilage and defectives in an engineering industry with special reference to the accounting treatment for each.
27. Distinguish between scrap, spoilage and defective work. How are they accounted for in the cost of products?
28. What do you understand by normal and abnormal waste of materials during process of manufacture? State briefly how each should be treated in cost accounts?
29. What is difference between normal wastage and abnormal wastage? How would you deal with each type of wastage?
30. Write short notes on the following:
    (a) Impress system of stores control
    (b) ABC method of stock control
    (c) Material handling

(d) Coding of materials
(e) Material transferred from one job to another
(f) Materials turnover
(g) Material requisition
(h) Quantity discount

31. Briefly explain the documents used in the process of material control.
32. Distinguish bind card from stores ledger.

LABOUR

1. Distinguish clearly between direct and indirect labour. What are the expenses which are normally classified an indirect labour in a manufacturing enterprise?
2. Distinguish between direct and indirect labour. State the methods of recovery of each in cost. What are the expenses which are normally classified as indirect labour in a manufacturing concern?
3. Discuss different methods of Time-keeping.
4. Discuss the various methods of recording attendance time.
5. Describe briefly the disc and time clock methods which you would recommend in a factory employing 1,000 men and why?
6. Discuss different methods of Time-booking.
7. What are the different types of job cards. Give their ruling and state in what circumstances each time is useful.
8. What are the advantages and disadvantages of the following ways recording labour time:

   (a) Daily time sheets (b) Weekly time sheets

   (c) Job cards accompanying each job through the work.
9. Distinguish between Time-keeping and Time-booking.
10. What is idle time? What are its causes? Suggest measures to reduce idle time.

11. What is meant by idle time? How is it treated in costing?
12. What do you understand by the term labour turnover? What are effects on efficiency of labour?
13. What do you understand by labor turnover? Enumerate the causes of such labour turnover and indicate some steps, which may reduce labour turnover.
14. What are the relative advantages of time rate and piece rate systems of remunerating labour?
15. "Time is the yardstick to measure the amount of service rendered by the laborers. Therefore, the payment by time is the most feasible method of wage payment". Critically examine the statement with special reference to advantages and defects of time wage system.
16. What do you mean by good plan of incentive wage payment? Explain the various premium or bonus methods of payment to workers.
17. Describe briefly the following methods of remunerating labour.
18. Distinguish between profit sharing and co-partnership as methods of remunerating labour.
19. Discuss the merits and demerits of the group incentive system of wage payment in a mass production factory.
20. What is a group bonus? Where can it be usefully employed? Describe briefly the features of group bonus systems.
21. Write short notes on:
    (a) Over-time (b) Casual workers
    (c) Out workers (d) Wages abstract

OVERHEADS

1. Define overhead and mention the different methods of classified of overhead.
2. Define "Cost classification". What are the methods of classification of overheads?

3. What are the broad heads under which various items of overhead expenses can be grouped? Give examples.
4. Overhead expenses fall into various groups, name these groups and give examples of the expenses of which they are comprised.
5. Distinguish between cost apportionment and overhead absorption.
6. Write notes on the following giving examples:
   (a) Cost classification (b) Cost allocation
   (c) Cost apportionment
7. Explain the meaning and classification of overheads suggest suitable bases with examples, for apportionment of overheads to departments.
8. Mention the broad principles on which overhead expenses are generally apportioned.
9. On what basis would you allocate the following costs to individual costs centers in a general engineering works?
   (a) Retests (b) Power
   (c) Lighting (d) Fire insurance
   (e) Depreciation of plant and machinery
   (f) Timekeeping expenses (g) Repairs
   (h) audit fees (i) Tabulation expenses
   (j) Delivery expenses
   (k) Fire precaution expenses
   (l) Steam
   (m) Canteen expenses.
10. What is meant by departmentalization of overhead expenses? What are its advantages?
11. What is meant by departmentalization of overhead expenses? What are the advantages of such departmentalization?
12. Enumerate the advantages of departmentalization of overhead expenses.

13. What do you understand by "departmentalization of overheads"? Why and how this is done?
14. Discuss the different methods of allocating overheads indicating the conditions, in which each method can be suitably used.
15. Explain the various methods of allocating factory on cost.
16. Describe various methods of calculating on cost. Explain their respective advantages and disadvantages.
17. Discuss fully the advantages and disadvantages of the following methods of overhead cost allocation.
    (i) Percentage method (ii) Labor hour method
18. Discuss different methods of overhead absorption.
19. How and why do you distinguish between fixed and variable overheads?
20. What do you understand by fixed and variable expenses? Why is it important to distinguish between two types of expenses? Give some examples.
21. Give arguments for and against inclusion of interest in expenses.
22. Enumerate the arguments for and those against the inclusion of interest on capital in the cost accounts.
23. What do you understand by over-recovery and under-recovery of expenses? Explain the causes and the method of dealing with both.
24. What is meant by depreciation and how is it dealt in cost accounts?
25. Differentiate depreciation from obsolescenes and explain the treatment of both those items in cost accounts.
26. Draft a form of plant and machinery register. State the advantages of maintaining such register.
27. How will you treat the following items of expenses in cost accounts?
    (a) Packages and Empties (b) Carriage
    (c) Interest on Capital (d) Bonus to Workers

28. How will you treat the following expenses in cost accounts?
    (a) Overtime wages
    (b) Cost of moulds in factory
    (c) Fire insurance
    (d) Purchasing department expenses
    (e) Internal transport costs.

29. How will you deal the following items of expenses in cost accounting?
    (a) Rent (b) Scrap
    (c) Tool-room expenses
    (d) Power house expenses (e) Leave pay.

30. How will you treat the following items of expenses in cost accounts?
    (a) Depreciation and obsolescence
    (b) Bad debts
    (c) Advertising
    (d) Rent, where premises are owned by the company.

31. How will you treat the following expenses in cost accounts?
    (a) Insurance on inventories;
    (b) Royalty on production;
    (c) Overtime wages;
    (d) Annual bonus to workers;
    (e) Repairs to machines.

32. How will you treat the following expenses in cost accounts?
    (a) Directors, fees and salaries
    (b) Cost office expenses
    (c) Market research
    (d) Research and development expenses.

SINGLE OR OUTPUT COSTING

1. Define costing.
2. Define Cost Accountancy.
3. Define Cost Accounting.
4. What is Cost?
5. Define the term Financial Accounting.
6. Define Management Accounting.
7. Define "Cost Unit".
8. Define "Cost Centre".
9. What are the functions of Cost Accounting?
10. What are the objectives of Costing?

CONTRACT COSTING

1. What is contract costing?
2. Explain the treatment of work-in-progress in contract accounts?
3. What is sub-contract cost?
4. What is meant by escalation clause?
5. What is cost plus contract?
6. Define target costing?
7. What is meant by retention money?
8. Explain the treatment of plant and machinery in contract accounts?
9. Explain briefly the treatment of profit on incomplete contracts.

JOB AND BATCH COSTING

1. What is job costing?
2. What is batch costing?
3. What is a job cost sheet? Give its model form.
4. What is Economic Batch Quantity?
5. What are the basic differences between contract costing and job costing?

PROCESS COSTING

1. What is meant by Process Costing?
2. What do you understand by the term "Normal Process Loss"?
3. What is abnormal loss? How is it treated the process accounts?
4. What is abnormal gain? How will you treat the same in cost records?
5. What are equivalent units?
6. What is Joint Product?
7. Define By-Product?
8. What do you mean by Co-products?
9. Mention the salient features of process costing?
10. What do you understand by the term inter process profits? Dicuss its importance in Process Costing?
11. How is Process Costing different from Job Costing?
12. Discuss the general features of process costing? Name the type of industries in which it is applied?
13. Explain Joint Products, and By-products. What are the methods generally used to account for these products?

RECONCILIATION OF COST AND FINANCIAL ACCOUNTS

1. Why is reconciliation of cost and financial accounts necessary?
2. What are the reasons for disagreement between the profit as per cost and financial accounts?
3. Write Accounts and cost accounts.
4. Write a note on Memorandum Reconciliation Account?
5. Explain how over-absorption and under-absorption of overheads will affect financial list out the various items which may appear in financial accounts?
6. Discuss the accounting procedure that is usually adopted in order to reconcile cost and financial accounts at the end of an accounting period.

7. In what ways will the profit reconciliation statement be useful to the management? Give proforma profit reconciliation statement.

MARGINAL COSTING

1. What is meant by "Direct Costing" or Marginal Costing? Describe its salient features in practice.
2. What do you understand by Marginal Costing? Discuss its usefulness and limitations.
   (a) What do you mean by marginal costing? Enumerate some of the advantages of the system.
   (b) Explain 'marginal costing' and set out the argument for and against it.
3. "The technique of marginal costing is a valuable aid to management". Discuss the statement and gibe your own views.
4. What is marginal costing? Enumerate the circumstances under which reduction of selling prices below total cost could be justified.
   (a) Under what circumstances may selling prices be reduced to marginal cost below marginal cost level.
5. Discuss the importance of the following terms in relation to marginal costing.
6. What do you understand by break-even chart? What are its advantages?
7. Explain the term "Break-even point". Give an example illustrating your answer
   (a) What do you understand by the term" Break-even point"? Who is it computed?
8. Calculate the break-even point from the following particulars?
9. What is meant by "cost-volume-profit analysis"? State the objectives of such analysis.
   (a) Define "cost-volume-profit analysis (C.V.P. analysis) and outline its uses and applications.

UNIFORM COSTING

1. What is meant by the term uniform costing?
2. What is meant by the term inter-firm comparison?
3. What is meant by uniform cost manual?
4. What are the objectives of 'inter-firm comparison'?
5. Define the term uniform costing. Give its advantages and limitations.
6. What are the pre-requisites to be considered while introducing the system of uniform cost in an industry?
7. What is uniform cost accounting system? What are the items on which you would seek uniformity so far as overheads are concerned in uniform cost accounting system?
8. What do you mean by inter-firm comparison? Give its advantages and limitations?
9. "A scheme of inter-firm comparison combines the advantages of a uniform costing system and benefits arising out of the use of ratios". Discuss.
10. You have been retained to advise on the introduction of a system of inter-firm comparison for a number of units in an industry. What are the essential points you would take care of to start with? Design your answer under the following heads:
    (a) The nature and extent of information to be collected.
    (b) The organisation to be set up for this purpose.
    (c) The method of collection, analysis and presentation of information.
11. Discuss the scope and application of uniform costing methods and their usefulness especially in the context of the economy of our country. Assume that you are advising a trade association in this regard in the interest of its member firms and outline you views and suggestions.

BUDGETARY CONTROL

1. What is budget?
2. What do you understand by budgetary control?
3. What is a budget center?
4. What is a budget manual?
5. What is budget committee?
6. What is budget period?
7. What is principal budget factor?
8. What is fixed budget?
9. What is meant by flexible budget?
10. What do you mean by functional budgets? Give examples.
11. What is Master budget?
12. What is Zero Base Budgeting?
13. What is summary budget?
14. Explain the procedure for the preparation of sales budget.
15. What are the essentials of an effective budgetary control system?
16. What factors are to be considered when preparing a purchase budget?
17. What is a flexible budget? What are its advantages?
18. Explain briefly what you understand by the following?
19. What do understand by budgetary control? Explain its disadvantages.

STANDARD COSTING

1. Define standard cost.
2. Define standard costing.
3. Explain the meaning of variance analysis.
4. Explain cost variance.
5. What is meant by material price variance?
6. Explain mix variance?

7. What is yield variance?
8. What is material usage variance?
9. What is labour cost variance?
10. What is labour rate variance?
11. What do you mean by labour efficiency variance?
12. What is idle time variance?
13. Differentiate between standard costs and estimated costs.
14. Distinguish between budgetary control and standard costing.
15. Distinguish between historical costing and standard costing.
16. Define standard costing. How is standard costs ascertained? Also state the advantages and disadvantages.

OPERATING OR SERVICE COSTING

1. With a mixed fleet of a hundred goods transport vehicles, how would you calculate an hourly rate for vehicle for charging to jobs and services?
2. State the advantages and disadvantages of using the following units for comparing the operating costs of road transport:
3. Prepare a power house cost statement and insert imaginary figures. What are the vital statistics required?
4. A brewery maintains a motor service consisting of twelve lorries, delivering barreled and bottled bear, and bringing back empties. Outline a system of cost control, covering the cost of running, maintenance and depreciation recommending the unit of measurement to be applied.
5. Draw up a performa cost statement for a canteen subsidized by the company, serving a firm of 5,000 employees. What measures of efficiency would you use in such a case and on what basis would canteen prices be fixed?
6. For a newly built 100 bed hospital attached to a big industrial under taking, briefly outline a procedure to

control receipts and issuers of medicines, etc. and cash receipts on the following management discussions:

(a) Employees will get all facilities free.

(b) Relatives and servants of employees will get free medicines from outdoor department only.

(c) Others will get facilities on payment only, rates of which should normally be 30 per cent higher than cost price to cover departmental charges.

7. Define 'operating costs' to what industries is this method of costing applicable.
8. Distinguish between operation costs and operating costs.

COST AUDIT

1. Explain the term cost audit
2. Explain (a) Proprietory Audit (b) Efficiency Audit.
3. What do you mean by internal audit?
4. What is statutory audit?
5. Explain briefly 'z' chart.
6. Distinguish between Financial Audit and Cost Audit?
7. Distinguish between proprietory audit and efficiency audit.
8. Discuss the functions of cost audit in a manufacturing organisation.
9. What are the objects of cost audit?
10. Explain the various types of cost audit.
11. What is a cost audit? What points would you look into if you embark on a cost audit programme? Also discuss the advantages of cost audit.
12. What principles will the cost accountant keep in mind while preparing and submitting his reports to the management?
13. What is uniform costing? What are the advantages and disadvantages of uniform costing?